THE COMPLETE GUIDE TO
MAKING WIRE JEWELRY

THE COMPLETE GUIDE TO
MAKING WIRE JEWELRY

Wing Mun Devenney

BARRON'S

A QUARTO BOOK

First edition for the United States, its territories and dependencies, and Canada published in 2015 by Barron's Educational Series, Inc.

All inquiries should be addressed to:
Barron's Educational Series, Inc.
250 Wireless Boulevard
Hauppauge, New York 11788
www.barronseduc.com

ISBN: 978-1-4380-0655-0

Library of Congress Control No. 2014956698

QUAR.JCBW

Conceived, designed, and produced by
Quarto Publishing plc
The Old Brewery
6 Blundell Street
London N7 9BH

Senior Editor: Lily de Gatacre
Art Director: Caroline Guest
Copy Editor: Liz Jones
Designer: Elizabeth Healey
Photographer: Phil Wilkins
Proofreader: Sarah Hoggett
Indexer: Helen Snaith
Creative Director: Moira Clinch
Publisher: Paul Carslake

Color separation in Hong Kong by Cypress Colours (HK) Ltd
Printed in China by 1010 Printing Limited

9 8 7 6 5 4 3 2 1

Publisher's Note

Wire jewelry making involves working with cutting tools, which are potentially hazardous and are used at your own risk. The guidelines laid down in this book are important, and should be read and followed carefully. Readers should also check their compliance with health and safety legislation currently in force, and always follow manufacturers' instructions, guidelines, and recommendations for using and storing tools and equipment. The publisher accepts no liability for loss or damage sustained in the course of using this book.

Contents:

Introduction

Wire has endless attractive qualities, which makes it an ideal material with which to create jewelry. Unlike traditional jewelry making, wire-constructed jewelry requires very few tools, and the techniques are easy to master. Wire-formed pieces can rival any conventionally constructed piece in their beauty, function, durability, and professional-quality finish. As you don't need much in the way of equipment, and only a simple workstation is necessary, using wire is a great place to start your adventures in jewelry making.

Enjoy the journey!

Wing Mun Devenney

Wing Mun Devenney

About this book

Chapter One: Getting Started, pages 8–23
All about the tools, equipment, and materials you will need, as well as an explanation of the design processes.

Chapter Two: Techniques, pages 24–103
Master a wide range of commonly used wire jewelry-making techniques, starting with pliers and small hand tools, and moving on to jigs for more complicated techniques and making identical multiples of the same design.

Chapter Three: Projects, pages 104–141
This chapter explores the creative applications of the techniques and skills presented in the previous chapter. The projects are contemporary in style but use traditional techniques and a mixture of commonly used materials and beads. Follow the project stages precisely or take inspiration and adapt, develop, and create your own personal designs.

Chapter Four: Pattern Directory, pages 142–155
A pattern directory containing finished samples and corresponding templates for a range of freehand and jig designs.

Note: Imperial and metric measurements
When making a project, follow either metric OR imperial measurements. Some of the measurements given are very small, so it would be ideal to work from the metric measurements. All conversions given are approximate.

From Chapter Two: Techniques

Detailed instructions that guide you through each technique

Clear step-by-step photographs

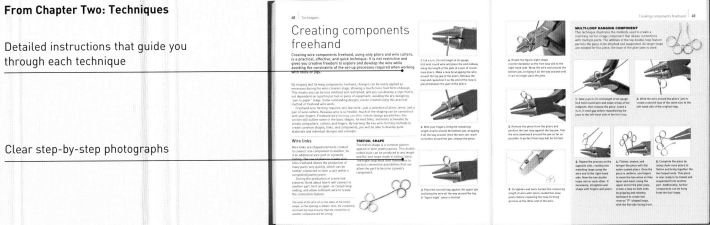

From Chapter Three: Projects

List of tools and materials, including precise quantities of wire and beads

Beautiful photography that showcases the finished piece

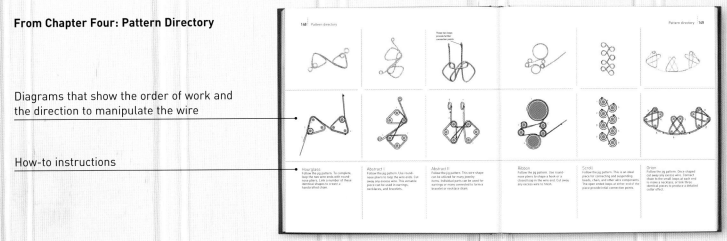

From Chapter Four: Pattern Directory

Diagrams that show the order of work and the direction to manipulate the wire

How-to instructions

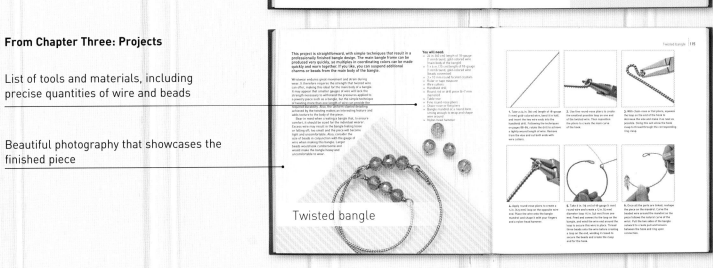

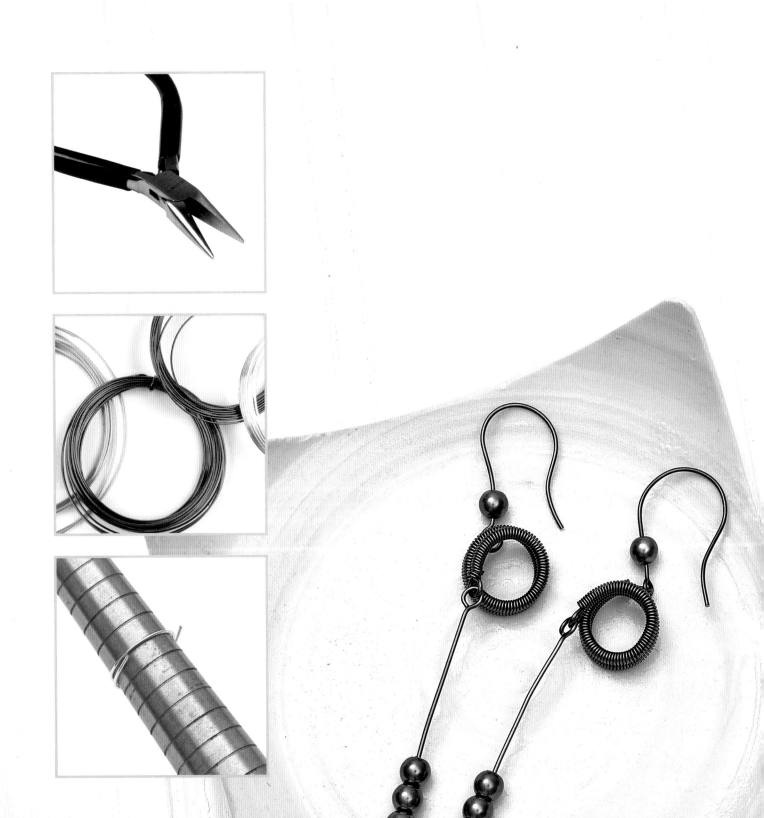

Chapter One:
Getting Started

Before starting jewelry making, it's important to make sure you know all about the necessary tools, equipment, and materials, as well as the design processes and the ideal work environment. This chapter will give you ideas on where to look for design inspiration, as well as a list of essential materials, types of equipment, storage options, and tips on how to optimize your work area for creating wire jewelry. The insights from this chapter will give you a rounded understanding of the basics before you move on to the Techniques and Projects chapters.

Design ideas and inspiration

Any successful jewelry designer and maker will possess a unique style and design signature. To develop a piece or collection, they will often gather inspiration from their surroundings—the natural environment, an architectural genre, or a fashion era of interest. There are many factors that can lead to the development of a particular design or style. Here are some of the things to think about when designing jewelry.

Design/Style

The design of any piece of jewelry is the primary factor to consider. Essentially a fashion accessory, a piece of jewelry can complement and "finish" an outfit.

Designers often take inspiration from where they are: an art gallery, a museum, or a walk in the country can all spark an idea. Design inspiration can also be derived from a particular interest, a technique, a particular material, or even a piece of equipment that the maker is attracted to. To begin, gather as much information as possible and consider subjects of personal interest: a historical period, a type of tree bark, the colors and patterns of sea shells, lines and shapes produced by everyday objects—the list of inspirational possibilities is endless. Magazines and books are also a valuable source of information, and you can maintain a sense of current style by reading through fashion and jewelry magazines. Travel opens the mind and is a catalyst for creativity, but don't feel you have to go far—even a walk around your local area can result in as many ideas as a trip to a faraway country.

Try to design according to the seasons to ensure that your jewelry pieces are appropriately matched to colors and styles. Bright, fresh colors may work better around spring and summer, while during the fall and winter months, richer tones and colors may be more suitable.

Finally, do not be frightened of creating signature pieces that fit with your own individual style—after all, that is what makes a designer unique. Embrace the techniques presented later in this book and adapt them to your own personal needs and individual preferences. Do what feels the most natural, follow or adapt techniques—and if you believe a design would benefit

This matching set was made using the same techniques as illustrated in the Bird's Nest Necklace project on pages 138–141.

from adjustments or personalized features, then change it as necessary to make the piece individual and unique.

Wearer

Aside from personal style, the comfort and needs of the potential wearer must also be considered. So who is the jewelry piece for? Give thought to the wearer's physique: If they are particularly tall, the piece may have to be longer, for instance. If the wearer is petite, the piece might be better suited to intricate detailing. Hair and skin coloring may also determine the stones, beads, and wire colors to use. The wearer's occupation could determine the practical requirements of the piece. A good designer will understand the wearer and take their needs into consideration to design suitable pieces for them.

Comfort

Comfort is extremely important to the success of a piece of jewelry. After all, jewelry is worn on the body and must fit both securely and comfortably. One thing you'll need to think about is the weight of the piece; for example, earrings must be lightweight or they could cause the wearer discomfort; a large group of heavy beads may look attractive, but it might be tiring to wear. Consider how a piece will drape off the wearer: will the length allowed be sufficient? Is the item heavier on one side so it will be pulled out of position? What arrangement of beads will look the best, while also remaining wearable?

Materials

The magic of jewelry making comes in part from the abundance of beautiful wires, beads, stones, and other components you have to choose from. A visit to any good jewelry supplies store can make you feel like you have entered Aladdin's cave filled with beads, findings, and chains of every color and size. It can be impossible to leave without amassing an array of small trinkets to be transformed into beautiful pieces of jewelry. Because of the variety of components on offer, design inspiration is often derived from the materials themselves. Perhaps a beautiful strand of beads, an interesting cut of stone, or a certain type of chain will inspire you to create an entire range of jewelry designs.

Experiment with different beads and metals and use these as design tools—mixing and matching, creating and designing, directly from the materials alone. As with any

Wire-wrapped beads have been secured along the length of this chain to create a colorful bracelet (above). The three pieces at right and below were created using hand-coiling techniques (see page 74).

By sketching out your ideas and designs, you can create a diagram to follow like a template to help you shape your wire.

creative medium, wire is there to be experimented with—so let it inspire you. Practice, learn, and improve. Place beads on a bead board and use it like a sketchbook, mixing colors and materials, beads, chains, findings, and so on to work out ideas.

There are no hard and fast rules to design and, ultimately, learning the techniques in this book will give you the skills to create any piece of wire jewelry, so do not be scared to experiment and fashion a piece that suits your own style and needs. Furthermore, do not restrict yourself to using only jewelry suppliers; many other stores are ideal places to gather parts, findings, beads, and stones. Be individual and create unique pieces using secondhand materials. A visit to a thrift or vintage store may deliver suitable jewelry items—retro jewelry pieces, coins and buttons, or small trinkets that can be dismantled and applied to new pieces in different ways. Haberdasheries are also ideal sources of materials such as ribbons, cords, leather, buttons, zippers, and fasteners, as well as many other metal components.

Collecting ideas

Once you have decided which interests to follow and taken other factors into consideration, you will need to document these influences in a sketchbook. Note down ideas and record the visuals that inspired you before starting to create sketches of potential designs. Inspiration can strike anywhere and at any time, so carry your sketchbook with you wherever you go. Perhaps a country walk will bring you colorful fall leaves, water lashing the seafront, or the textures of birds' feathers.

Before starting to create a piece, sketch out the idea in detail. If possible, make your sketch actual size so that you can use it as a guide. Exact measurements and colors can also be determined at this stage, and it is also useful to think about potential technical problems. At the design

stage, evaluate the piece and whether it can be easily made; are there areas where you will need to allow the wire ends to be hidden in order to complete the piece professionally? Does the wirework technique you plan to use coordinate with the materials and beads selected? These are just some of the questions a designer should ask during the pen-to-paper design stage. Furthermore, it might prove beneficial to test some of the techniques you plan to use before embarking on the production of the entire piece. With time you will become familiar with the properties of particular components and beads and more skilled in the techniques, allowing you to make informed design decisions more quickly.

Environment

To make wire jewelry, you don't need a lot of specialist equipment or an elaborate, dedicated workspace. However, to ensure you make your jewelry in the most suitable, comfortable environment, there are a few factors to consider.

A perfect wire jewelry-making area consists of a workstation in a bright space. The work surface should be large enough to accommodate and support your forearms, wrists, and hands. It should provide adequate space for all the necessary tools and jewelry parts. As most pieces of jewelry are of a manageable size, a large desk should offer ample space to work from; however, a larger table will offer greater flexibility, so a dining table can work really well, too. The surface of the desk should be smooth, flat, and white if possible; this will show off the jewelry materials' true colors.

In addition to the desk or table, a comfortable chair is essential. The height and position of the table and chair should be adjustable to offer the best support and comfort. Sit at the center of the desk so both arms and hands are supported, with space on either side to allow for movement during the manufacturing process, or when locating jewelry parts and tools. As so much of wire jewelry making relies on accurate measurements, it can be helpful to glue a tape measure along the edge of the table, close to where you work. This will allow you to record measurements as you work.

The table or desk should be located in a well-lit area. Jewelry parts tend to be quite small, so a brightly lit work area will allow you to see all the parts clearly, as well as to color match them. Natural light is best so, if possible, work near a window. However, if this is impossible, a desk lamp with a moveable angled head should be sufficient.

Frequently used tools, such as pliers and cutters, as well as regularly applied components, should be placed within easy reach. Always gather the tools and materials necessary for the piece you are working on and position them on the desk before you begin. This will save you time, and should help you avoid accidents or damage to a piece partway through the making process. Never use a tool that is unsuitable for a technique just because it's closer, as this may ruin the end result.

Findings and beads are best organized in clear, divided, closable storage containers. Categorize each storage container by bead type and color. Findings should also be organized according to the metal color and type. Wires on their reels or coils can be stored in a small drawer unit. Once a wire coil packet is opened, store the coils in resealable bags to keep the coil from becoming tangled. All findings, beads, wires, and other components are best positioned at the top end of the table, within easy reach. However, you'll find your own preferences for arranging your workstation— the best advice is to create an environment that is safe and comfortable and will allow for inspirational and creative, but practical use.

A bright, well-organized, and comfortable work area will make your jewelry making more comfortable and successful.

Keep your findings and beads organized and separated so that you can find exactly what you need easily and quickly.

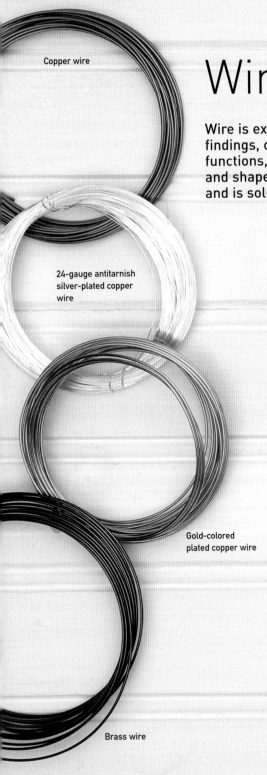

Copper wire

24-gauge antitarnish silver-plated copper wire

Gold-colored plated copper wire

Brass wire

Wire and other materials

Wire is extremely versatile. It can be shaped to form components and findings, or used to secure beads and stones. To fulfill its many possible functions, wire is available in a selection of gauges, colors, metal types, and shapes. It is readily available from good jewelry or craft suppliers, and is sold in lengths, coils, and spools.

Wire metal types and colors

Wire is available in both precious and nonprecious metals. Precious metal wires include platinum, palladium, gold, and silver. Although precious metal wire can be used for wirework jewelry, platinum and palladium can only be used for fine jewelry items that are heated and soldered, due to the cost and the hardness of the metal. Silver and gold are sufficiently malleable without being heated to allow for wire forming; however, due to the high cost of gold, silver remains the one precious metal that is commonly used in wire jewelry making.

Precious metal wire—Silver, gold, palladium, and platinum are all precious metals available in wire form. These precious wires are available in many shapes, sizes, and grades—for example, gold is available in 9ct, 14ct, 18ct, 22ct, and 24ct grades.

Silver- and gold-plated wire—Both gold- and silver-plated wires are available to buy from jewelry suppliers. They are relatively cheap, especially compared with solid precious metal wires. As both silver and gold are generally plated over copper, the wire itself is easy to work with. Due to its chemical properties, silver will discolor and tarnish over time, so it is advisable to buy antitarnish silver-plated wire.

Nonprecious wire—Brass, copper, and aluminum can all be used for wire jewelry; however, aluminum tends to be very soft, and the finish it offers is less refined compared with copper. Copper is extremely common in wire jewelry making—in particular, the colored, plated, or enameled versions. Brass is an inexpensive metal and is therefore often applied as a practice metal.

Craft jewelry wires/Colored copper wire—Craft wire as is popular with both crafters and jewelers; this is a color-coated copper wire. Available in many colors and gauges, this wire is both flexible and easy to work with. It is also affordable and easy to obtain, which makes it possibly the most popular nonprecious metal wire.

Preknitted wire—This can be cut to size and shaped, connected to other parts, or have beads attached to it. Available in many colors and wire gauges, and in sheet or tubular strand form for fancy knits, this type of material can be ideal for making large pieces of jewelry. Combined with findings and beads, knitted pieces can very quickly be made into finished pieces of jewelry.

Memory wire—Made in stainless steel and tempered so that it retains its shape, this wire is sold in various forms. Most common are the rounded, shaped coils, but memory wire is also available in circular and oval precut shaped bangles, rings, and neckpieces. Beads and other components can be added to swiftly achieve a finished jewelry piece.

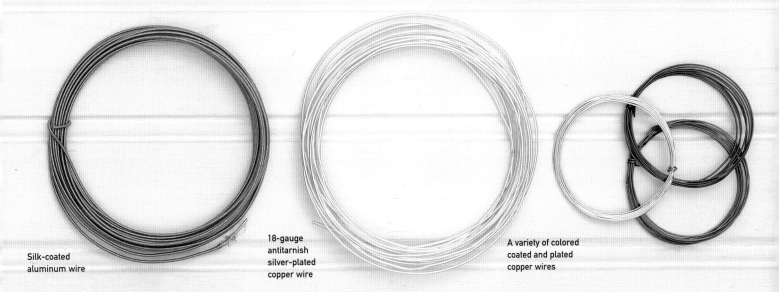

Silk-coated
aluminum wire

18-gauge
antitarnish
silver-plated
copper wire

A variety of colored
coated and plated
copper wires

Memory wire is available in several colors of plated finishes—gold, silver, and an antique dark rhodium finish. It also comes in round or flat wire sections. The wire can be shaped using ordinary pliers, though specially designed memory-wire pliers can also be used. Coils of memory wire can be cut to the desired length, but memory-wire cutters must be used for these; normal wire cutters will be unable to cut through the tough stainless steel and may be damaged in the process.

Beading wire—This wire is used to thread, connect, and secure beads. It is extremely resilient and flexible, and its nylon coating makes threading beads easy. There are many brands of beading wire available, each with their own features; however, they tend to be fairly similar. Beading wire is sold in spools and cut to size. Take care to use strong cutters, as normal cutters will be damaged. Choose beading wire according to the size of the drilled holes of the beads—the wire should fill most of the hole, but leave enough of a gap to allow the bead to thread onto it and move slightly.

The strand number denotes the number of internal wires that make up one strand of beading wire. The higher the number of internal strands, the greater a wire's flexibility and softness, making it ideal for smaller, lighter, and possibly more precious beads. For heavier beads and components, a lower strand number wire will offer greater support. As well as the gauge and strand number, beading wire will often be described by the spool length, the strength, color, or recommended use.

Tiger tail—Essentially, this is the same as beading wire, but much cheaper; it is less flexible and can easily become kinked and misshapen. Take care when using this type of beading wire.

Wire shape

There are many shapes of wire available. Round wire is possibly the most commonly used jewelry wire, for all kinds of jewelry. It is versatile, easy to shape and form, and readily available in many gauges, metal types, and colors. Although round-section wire is popular, square-, rectangular-, and D-section wires are also good to use. You can also find triangular- and oval-section wire.

Wire size/Gauge

Wire size is measured by the diameter of the section, given by gauge in the US and in millimeters in European countries. "GA" is the abbreviation for gauge; the higher the gauge, the smaller the diameter of the wire. The variety of wire gauges allows for many possible techniques. The thicker and heavier the gauge, the more difficult it is to shape and work, but the stronger and more durable the piece will become. Therefore, using heavier-gauge wire for larger pieces that are prone to greater stress is ideal, while using much thinner and higher gauges of wire for delicate parts is most suitable.

32–28-gauge/0.2–0.3 mm—This is extremely fine and delicate wire, and is suitable for knitting, crocheting, and the binding of parts. Care should be taken when knitting with this gauge of wire, as it can easily snap; to avoid this happening, it is best to create quite loose knits.

26-gauge/0.4 mm—Although this gauge is not as narrow as 32–28, it is still suitable for crochet and knit work. It can also work well for binding and securing parts and beads in a piece, using the wire wrapping technique.

24-gauge/0.5 mm—This works well for knitting work such as Viking weave; it can also be used for head-/eye-pin production, as well as for securing beads or stones. It can be an ideal size for wire macramé (see page 86).

22–20-gauge/0.6–0.8 mm—Possibly the most commonly used sizes of wires. These are versatile wires that are suitably sized for making findings, and they can be easily wound, shaped, and formed into many different designs.

18–16-gauge/1–1.3 mm—At this size, wire starts to become much harder to manipulate, as it is firmer and thicker; however, this is ideal—and strong enough—to form clasps, heavier shapes, and it retains its shape better.

14-gauge/1.5 mm—Any size wire upward of this gauge is quite thick, and without annealing and heating is increasingly difficult to shape. However, this is a practical width to shape frames or main centerpieces to which parts will be secured. Additionally, this, or a heavier gauge, would be ideal for creating shaped forms such as bangles, neckpieces, and torques.

Wire hardness

The hardness of a wire determines its flexibility. The stiffer the wire, the harder it is to bend and manipulate. Of course, the softer the wire, the easier it will be to form.

Dead-soft wire is extremely soft and pliable, and can be formed using your hands alone. Easily contorted, this wire is excellent for multiple coiled and wrapped wire shapes, in addition to bead wrapping. The disadvantage of using soft wire is that the finished piece can very easily become misshapen if badly handled.

Half-hard wire is slightly stiffer than dead-soft wire. Half-hard wire is excellent for making tight, angular bends, wire loops, and for wrapping around itself.

Hard wire is very stiff, but once formed, a wire piece is more likely to retain its shape.

No single wire is perfect for all applications. Soft wire is easy to bend and shape, but the finished product may deform. Hard wire is difficult to bend, but makes permanent shapes. Half-hard wire is a compromise between the two, and once a shape is formed the piece can be tempered by hammering, working with pliers, or polishing; doing this will help the piece to retain its shape.

Choosing wire

Most of the projects and techniques in this book have been created using color-plated copper wire. This choice is based on many things: its malleable qualities, its cost effectiveness, its ready availability, and the vast range of sizes and color-plated finishes on offer.

Plated or coated copper wire is very attractive for jewelry-making purposes, in particular the antitarnish silver-plated wire. This wire has the appearance of silver but does not tarnish, so the finished piece will not become discolored—it is my ideal wire of choice.

Beads

A bead is a small, decorative component with a hole drilled through it to allow for threading. Commonly sold in strands or in bagged quantities, there are many types of beads available—almost any shape, color, size, or type of bead can be found. Match the beads to the wire or cord color to enhance your piece.

Precious—Precious beads are cut from natural stones and tend to be expensive, so are usually only used for fine jewelry. There are many types of precious beads and pearls.

Semiprecious—Semiprecious beads may be inexpensive, but many types are also quite valuable.

Metal beads—An array of base-metal beads is available in a variety of colors, shapes, and finishes.

Crystal—Faceted and cut to mimic precious stones and formed with lead glass, these beads have high reflective qualities. Stronger and more precious than glass, crystal beads are extremely popular and are available in many colors and shapes.

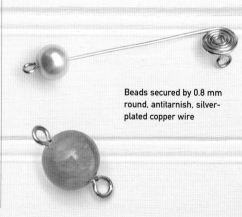

Beads secured by 0.8 mm round, antitarnish, silver-plated copper wire

Plastic—Plastic beads are truly modern jewelry components. They allow for designs of any color or size, and are fun, cost-effective, and easy to obtain.

In addition, any good jewelry supplier will be able to offer beads created from materials such as wood, ceramic, glass, textiles, and natural seeds.

Stones

Natural stones can be obtained in many forms and cuts. Many natural semiprecious stones are ideal for combining with wire, and can instantly add character and value to a wire-jewelry piece.

Chains

Chains are often employed in jewelry making, and can be used to suspend pendants and centerpieces, or to connect components together. As with wires, there are many types of chains available, formed from a range of metal types, styles, colors, and lengths. Here are some of the most common:

Curb—A hugely popular chain style, the links of this interlock with each other when laid flat.

Trace—Again, a popular and common chain; the links are equal in width and length.

Ball—Fashioned from individual ball units that are connected by a central pin.

Snake—Composed of very closely connected links that form a tubular length in a square or round shape. This type of chain has a very fluid nature and when worn will sit closely against the wearer, following the form of their body.

Box—Created from square-shaped links; a contemporary style of chain.

Crystal—Formed of individual claw-set crystal stones that are connected by a central metal tab. Ideal for areas that require the display of multiple crystals.

Nonmetal cords

Jewelry can often include nonmetal components such as the following.

Jewelry thread—Like beading wire, jewelry thread is used to thread and connect a length of beads. It is available in both nylon and silk, although nylon is usually used because it is cheaper and more flexible and durable.

Leather, suede, and other cords—There are many bracelets and neckpieces finished with leather, suede, or textile cords. Available in many sizes, shapes, and colors, these options are attractive materials to combine with metal. They are readily available from both jewelry suppliers and haberdasheries, and can be mixed with multicolored beads for a contemporary look. They are also easy to connect using end caps, findings, or intricate knotting methods.

Elastic—Elastic is an ideal material for easy-to-wear bracelets. Available in many colors, the elastic can be matched easily to the beads it is securing. Elastic is ideal for children's jewelry; however, it is much less durable than metal beading wire. Elastic thread is a good stringing material for beginner jewelers, though; it is extremely easy to use, no additional findings are required, and charms and beads can be easily threaded, connected, and secured in place. It is sold on reels and is quite cheap.

Ribbon/Satin—Ribbons are available in many sizes, shapes, and colors, as well as in different materials. Affordable, easy to obtain, and in a wide range of styles, ribbon is a very desirable jewelry-making material.

Invisible wire/Illusion cord—This wire is often used by jewelers to create pieces that appear as if the threaded beads are suspended in midair. Beads are held in particular positions with the help of glue or crimps. Invisible wire is also used for threading translucent beads.

Silicone wire—A plastic-based cord that gives a modern aesthetic to a piece of jewelry, this option is available in many colors and gauges, and is sold in lengths.

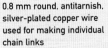

0.8 mm round, antitarnish, silver-plated copper wire used for making individual chain links

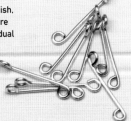

Findings

Findings are a family of jewelry components that are necessary to complete a piece. They are essentially any parts of a jewelry piece other than the chain and main components. The table below shows some that are used in this book.

NAME	USE	NAME	USE
Crimps	Small metal tubes or hollow beads that are squeezed at a desired position to secure parts or wire in place. A must for beading and stringing jewelry.	Cones	Shaped metal cones applied to cover areas of woven or strung items such as the end of a knit piece.
Crimp covers	Spherical metal covers used to hide unsightly crimps.	Cord and cap ends	Cord and cap ends—used to cover and secure cord, leather, ribbon, etc.
Calottes	Domed, two-part covers that are used to hide beading wire, thread knots, or crimps.	Folded-over ribbon ends	Used to cover cord ends by folding tab ends over the cord to secure it in place. Often available with a loop-ended option so that further connection is possible.
Wire guards	U-shaped metal components with tubular ends to allow wire beading wire to fit through. Wire guards protect beading wire at a point of connection between two components and are available in various sizes and metal colors.	Clasps: bolt, lobster	There are many different types of clasps, in a variety of metal types and sizes; a selection is made according to the design and weight of the final jewelry piece it is to connect.
French wire	Like wire guards, French wire protects beading wires and threads at the point of connection and friction. It is sold in lengths and cut to size when required.		
Head pins	Extremely common—used to secure beads and charms. They are composed of a length of wire with a head that keeps threaded components from falling off.	Split rings	Closed, double-coiled, round wire loops that are used for connections. Split rings are much stronger than jump rings.
Ear wire	Threaded through pierced ears and can be curved in round or hoop shapes. Available in open- and closed-back versions.	Jump rings	Open-ended, round wire rings, used to connect parts together.

Tools

Good tools are essential for making jewelry precisely and accurately. There is a huge range of jewelry-making tools and equipment available to buy, but for wire jewelry you can manage with a few high-quality basics to start with and build up from there. This section shows you the essentials. It begins with an introduction to the most commonly used tools and equipment, then moves on to the tools you will need to create more advanced pieces.

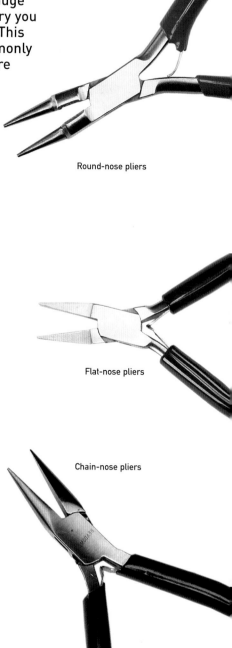

Round-nose pliers

Flat-nose pliers

Chain-nose pliers

Pliers

Pliers are probably the most frequently used jewelry tools, especially in the production of wire jewelry. There are many types available, and understanding their individual properties will help you make the right choice.

In addition to a variety of shapes of jaws, pliers are also available in different sizes, and with and without spring-action and rubber-coated handles. Spring-handled pliers reduce the amount of hand stress endured during wirework; there is quite a substantial amount of repetitive hand action required, so this can be desirable. Rubber-handled pliers also offer a more secure grip and greater support; this also reduces the amount of stress the hands will experience during repetitive wirework. Reduced hand stress will allow you to work for longer periods.

Round-nose pliers—These are possibly the most useful and most utilized tool in wire jewelry making. They are ideal for making curved shapes, bends, and loops. As the jaws of these taper, various sizes of loops are achievable; however, if a number of identical loops are required, it is best to mark the position of the jaws in order to replicate the exact size. Round-nose pliers are the most flexible pliers to use, because they have the ability to shape and form wire without marking and damaging the piece, and they allow for easy bending and twisting. Short-nose versions offer greater strength and stability, while longer-nose pliers are better able to reach awkward areas.

Flat-nose pliers—These pliers have matching, rectangular-shaped jaws that can hold and bend angular, sharp corners. The large surface area of the jaws offers a strong grip on wires, as well as the capability to flatten and straighten.

Chain-nose pliers—Chain-nose pliers, with their tapering flat jaws, are ideal to grip and hold wire, to shape and form, and to open and close jump rings, as well as to press and secure crimps in place. Chain-nose pliers can secure crimps, but they will not offer a professionally finished crimp when compared with using crimping pliers (see page 20). Due to the sharp, tapered jaws, these pliers are particularly useful for getting into small areas. Chain-nose pliers, as the name suggests, are useful in chain making because they grip and open links to allow for connection.

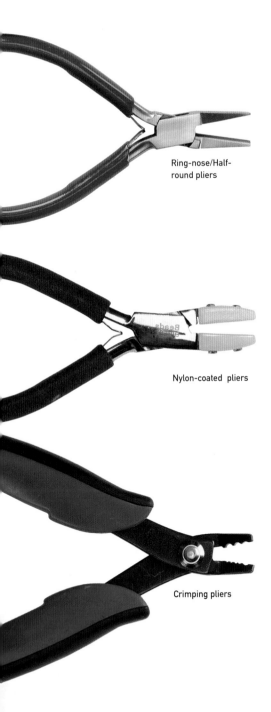

Ring-nose/Half-round pliers

Nylon-coated pliers

Crimping pliers

Ring-nose/Half-round pliers—With one flat and one rounded jaw, these pliers shape and form ring shanks, earring wires, and any other curved parts. Half-round pliers also help with the reshaping of rounded, curved shapes that have been created on a wire jig and may have become slightly distorted while being removed from the pegs.

Curved chain-nose pliers—The jaws of these pliers are effectively chain-nose versions that have been curved in a forward angle. As these are tapered and bent, the jaws offer ease of access to difficult areas in addition to a strong grip. They are particularly useful in the opening and closing of small loops and jump rings.

Nylon-coated pliers—The jaws of these pliers are covered in nylon and prevent marking or damage to metal—in particular, wire. Flat-nose versions of these pliers are often applied to straighten and temper lengths of wire, though other profiles are also available.

Crimping pliers—These are specifically designed to squash and fold crimps. These pliers' jaws are devised with two channels: one at the back that squeezes the crimp downward into a "U" shape. This "U"-shaped crimp is then inserted into the front channel, which then folds it in half, shaping it into a neat and secure crimp. Do buy good-quality crimping pliers, as lower-cost options will only create an amateur-looking crimp.

Split ring opening pliers—With one normal tapering jaw and one bent-nose tip, these pliers hold and pry open the rings of a split ring to allow for connection.

Tip: It is useful to own more than one pair of the same shape of pliers in different sizes.

Wire cutters

As with pliers, there are various types of wire cutters. Make sure to select the correct version for the type of cutting you are doing so as to prevent damage to the piece—and to avoid destroying the cutters themselves. An inappropriate selection can cause fine flush cutters' jaws to become marked and damaged.

Side cutters—Side cutters have jaws that meet at an angle. They are used for cutting heavier-gauge wire (thicker than 24-gauge/1 mm).

Flush cutters—With angled cutting jaws, flush cutters are similar to side cutters but are able to cut finer jewelry wires. Due to the side-cutting properties, this type of cutter is able to trim and remove small areas and parts. Flush cutters are side cutters that offer a more refined cut, though; they are available in several grades, and generally the higher the cost, the straighter and neater the cut.

End cutters—The jaws of these cutters meet at a straight angle, perpendicular to the body. The position of the jaws makes these cutters ideal for removing protruding wire ends or for cutting heavy-gauge wires. Note that these cutters will not permit access to small areas and are therefore not often used for fine wirework.

Memory-wire cutters—Memory-wire cutters offer the strength and support to cut into stainless-steel memory wire. Do not use ordinary wire cutters to cut memory wire, as they will be damaged.

Tip: Beading wire can also be composed of quite durable, strong metal, so do take care to cut it with suitable strong cutters.

Mandrels

A mandrel is a tool around which metal or wire can be formed and shaped. There are many different sizes, shapes, and material types to choose from.

Makeshift mandrel—Various household objects can be transformed into a mandrel. Any object that has a strong body can be used, whether metal rods, ends of drill bits, wooden craft dowels, food tins and jars, wooden or metal kitchen utensil handles, bottles, etc... the list is endless. Regardless of the object chosen, do ensure it is strong enough to withstand the wrapping of wire and that it is secured and stabilized during use.

Ring mandrel/Triblet (1)—Ring mandrels, also commonly known as triblets, are available in steel, aluminum, and wood. The section of a ring mandrel is normally round, and the body itself tapers or steps in size to allow multiple loop or curve sizes to be created—larger sizes near the base and gradually smaller up to the top end of the mandrel. Some ring mandrels show ring sizes for ease of reference. As well as coming in different materials, ring mandrels also come in different sizes.

NOTE: Do take care, when purchasing a ring mandrel, that it is actually a mandrel and not a ring stick. Although a ring stick looks the same as a ring mandrel, it is only designed for measurement of rings rather than as a former to shape metal against.

Bangle mandrel (2)—Bangle mandrels, similar to the ring versions, are tapering or stepped in size along the body of the piece to allow multiple sizes to be achieved. They are normally made from steel or wood, and are also available in various sizes.

NOTE: Tapering mandrels offer the ability to create multiple sizes; however, stepped mandrels, although unable to produce as many sizes, can be used to form uniform wire coils or shaped flat pieces of metal.

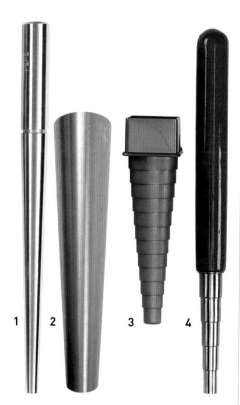

Multi-mandrel (3)—Multi-mandrels have a selection of different-shaped interchangeable heads to allow for various sizes and forms.

Jump-ring mandrel (4)—There are many jump-ring mandrels available, composed of straight metal bars or as stepped tapering versions, either of which allows for the coiling of wire to produce jump rings. These mandrels are normally available in multiple-size sets.

Tip: Mandrels can be held in place by hand or, if metal versions are used, secured to a table top with the help of a bench vise system.

More advanced tools

Planishing hammer—Planishing hammers are often used to smooth and flatten metal, but they are also ideal for hammering and stretching the ends of wires. The smooth and flat metal head can flatten, taper, and spread wire, which is useful when making brooch pins.

Nylon-coated/Rawhide hammer—Nylon- or rawhide-head hammers shape and manipulate metal and wire without stretching and distorting the piece. These hammers do not misshape or mark the metal on contact, so they are ideal for use against a mandrel for formation and shaping. They can also be used to temper a constructed wire piece against a metal flat plate to help it retain its shape.

Steel bench block—These are commonly used in fine jewelry for hammering techniques such as planishing and spreading of metal, or to temper a piece with a nylon-coated or rawhide hammer. A bench block provides a smooth and strong surface that a piece can be held against for hammering.

Handheld/Woodwork drill—Although an electric drill can be used, a woodwork hand drill is safer to use and offers greater control. Also, when used to secure a wire or wires at the chuck area, a hand drill provides the uniform and firm rotations required to twist single or multiple wires.

Pin vise—Traditionally used for jewelry making and watchmaking, a pin vise is a handy tool for making small sections of twisted wire. These miniature drill systems have interchangeable collets that allow the insertion of various-sized drill bits or wires. Once one or more wires are inserted they can be secured in place, ready for twisting. This tool is ideal for quick results, or for twisting small lengths, and can access and twist parts that are preconnected; however, for large, lengthy, or multiple strands of wires, a handheld drill will give greater support and better results.

Ring-holder clamp vise—Although initially designed to hold rings secure in various positions, this tool is now used to grip small pieces that are difficult to clasp with fingers alone. This tool is effectively a mini vise system with wooden- or leather-coated jaws that are strong but do not mark the metal, making it an ideal device for holding wire in place while it is being worked on.

Jewelry files—Jewelry files come in many shapes and sizes designed to fit into small or large areas to remove metal. They eliminate rough edges and marks and are essential in all kinds of jewelry making. For wirework, fine needle files are practical for removing sharp edges from cut wires. Good-quality jewelry files will outperform cheaper versions, so bear this in mind when choosing what to buy.

Jewelry saw and saw blades—A jewelry saw is lightweight and is specifically designed to hold fine saw blades that cut into metal, creating the finest of details and reaching into the tightest of spaces. To create professionally shaped and cut jump rings, a jewelry saw is essential.

Cup burr—A cup burr is a handheld tool with a metal cup-shaped file end. Wire is inserted into the cup, then the handle is rotated in clockwise and counterclockwise directions to round off and remove sharp edges—for example, on earring wires. Cup burrs are available in single-sized handheld versions, or as an interchangeable variable-head-size option.

Wire forming tools

Wire forming jig—A wire jig consists of a base board with holes drilled across the surface area, in which various sized and shaped pegs are inserted in different pattern configurations. Once a peg pattern is created, wire is then wound and shaped around the pegs to create uniform and repetitive forms and precisely shaped wire pieces.

Wire coiling tool—There are several types of wire coiling tools available, and each system is slightly different. However, the basics are that wire is secured to a central metal rod, which is then rotated. The winding action creates lengths of uniformly sized coils that can be used to make jump rings, be used as jewelry components, or be further coiled, shaped, and formed to created detailed jewelry parts.

Wire crinkle-shape maker—This is a simple acrylic three-part tool that creates lengths of zigzagged or wavy-patterned wires. It is simple, cheap, and very useful.

Wire spiral maker—This is a small acrylic tool that transforms lengths of wire into round, evenly shaped flat spirals. There are also specific jig pegs that fit particular jigs to permit the production of even wire spirals.

French knitting tool—This is a spool with protruding pins that wool or wire can be coiled around and "knitted" to create lengths of French knit.

Crochet hook—Traditionally used with yarn, this needle is an adaptable alternative to the plastic needle supplied with traditional French knitting spools. The strong, hooked end works well with wire.

Additional tools and materials

Tape measures/Ruler—Without accurate measurements, it would be almost impossible to work with wire. It is always best to try to calculate the amount of wire required so you can replicate a design. A ruler is normally sufficient, because jewelry pieces tend to be small in size, but for a larger piece a tape measure can be helpful.

Bench vise—A basic bench vise is installed on a table or bench top and has two jaws that secure parts in place. Vises are extremely useful for wire jewelry making, as they have the ability to secure wire during twisting or macramé techniques. A multi-angled vise can offer the benefit of an adjustable-jawed head.

Jewelry files

Ring-holder clamp vise

Wire jig

Planishing hammer

Bead trays—As beads are usually round, they have a tendency to roll, and therefore a bead tray offers both support and a method of design. Most beads trays have multiple compartments to house loose beads, as well as channeled sections for designing bead strands. The grooved channels are also marked with measurements, so you can determine finished lengths while you are positioning the beads.

Masking tape—A jeweler's toolbox is incomplete without masking tape. Its adhesive quality is strong enough to hold parts together, but it can also be removed easily from metal, wire, beads, and other components. It can also be used to cover and protect vulnerable areas or surfaces during production.

Vernier calipers—Calipers are used to accurately measure small parts and areas. The main feature is the slideable arm, which when opened allows the insertion of parts for measurement. Some calipers also offer dual slideable arms, which enable you to measure internal spaces, such as the internal diameter of a wire loop, the inside of a drilled hole, or the internal width of a ring band. Calipers are available in manual and digital versions.

Emery boards/papers—Emery boards and papers are extremely helpful for smoothing rough edges and wire ends. Keep a variety of grades on hand. To remove file marks or to smooth a marked area, always start with a coarse option and work up to a higher grade to achieve a smooth finish.

Soft polishing cloth—These can be used to straighten and temper wire, or to polish or clean a finished wire piece.

Nonslip mat or cloth—These offer a secure base for using certain pieces of jewelry-making equipment, such as the wire crinkle-shape maker.

Ring sizer stick/Ring gauge—Ring gauges are used to determine the wearer's ring size.

Protective eye gear—As with any type of practical work that requires the use of wire and tools, accidents can occur. To prevent injury to the eye, protective eyewear should be worn. Always take care when cutting the ends of a wire to cover the area to keep loose metal from flying toward the face or eye.

Lighter or thread zap—These can be applied to the ends of cords or ribbons to seal and prevent unraveling, before the piece is capped or secured to a metal component. It also makes for a more stable area for adhesion.

Glues—In many instances, a selection of glues is necessary to combine nonmetal materials and components with metal parts. Two-part epoxy or jewelry-friendly glues are essential. Always follow the manufacturer's advice and instructions.

Storage—Correct storage of tools and jewelry parts is essential to safeguard the tools and help you find beads and components quickly. Pliers must be stored with their jaws pointing upward to avoid damage. There are many jewelry storage units available to house beads, findings, and other components—making them easy to see and access.

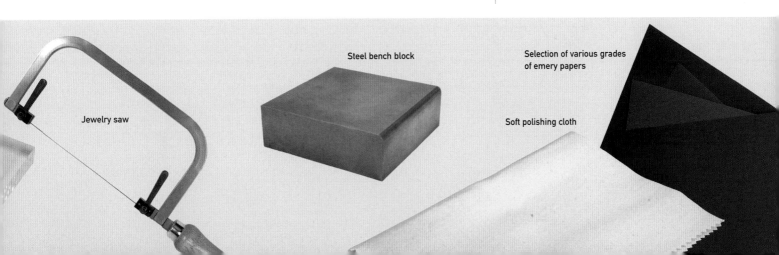

Jewelry saw

Steel bench block

Selection of various grades of emery papers

Soft polishing cloth

Chapter Two:
Techniques

This chapter will guide you as you master a wide range of commonly used wire jewelry-making techniques. It begins with simple techniques that use a selection of pliers and small hand tools, then moves on to more advanced equipment and jigs that will help you carry out more complicated techniques.

These techniques, along with a knowledge of how to use particular tools, will enable you to create many varied designs, to replicate pieces to create collections of jewelry, and perhaps most important, to develop your own techniques and to repair or adapt existing pieces you may already have and cherish. Follow the techniques: Copy, practice, and gain confidence so as to develop your own personal style.

Work hardening wire

Work hardening (tempering) is a process by which metal is pulled, bent, twisted, or hammered to make it stiffer. This manipulation brings the metal molecules closer together, making it harder and stronger, and less likely to be pulled apart or deformed during the production process or when worn. As well as retaining its shape, work-hardened wire will also have the springiness and tension required for jewelry parts such as hook clasps or brooch pins.

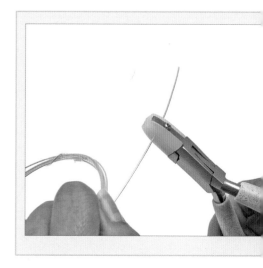

Work hardening can take place before the wire is used or once the piece has been finished; however, to work harden a finished piece may require more gentle manipulation. It is often advisable to work harden wire to a certain degree before work begins to give it the strength to retain shapes or remain straight, and also because it can be difficult to access parts of the completed piece.

Avoid overworking the wire; this could cause the metal to become brittle and weak, or even to break. As you do more work with metal, you will learn to recognize when a piece of wire is sufficiently work hardened.

Before tempering any wire, consider that work hardening can occur naturally as you manipulate the jewelry in the process of making it. Some wire-making techniques, such as coiling, require that the wire is soft and malleable, and in this case it should not be work hardened prior to construction of the piece. As you gain experience, it will become apparent when wire should be work hardened. Essentially, any piece that is created using a lot of movement should not require prior hardening.

Note: The hand-pull technique has the advantage of straightening the wire and removing any kinks or distorted sections prior to use. Hand-straightening wire can be extremely accurate, as fingers are so sensitive.

HAND PULL

This simple technique will allow you to easily feel the tension and rigidness created from each pull and to instinctively recognize when to stop the process. Uncoil a length of wire and, holding the coil and the wire, wrap a soft cloth around the top end before pulling along the length.

Repeat this several times, and the wire should become more rigid and straightened. This technique can be carried out with or without the soft cloth.

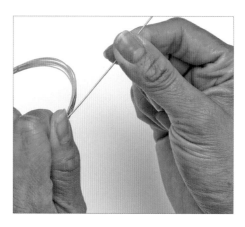
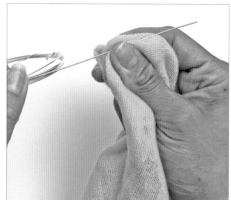

Cutting and rounding off wire

Jewelry wire is commonly sold in reels or coils, depending on the gauge and length. You can work with wire directly from the reel or coil, or cut precise lengths. Any cutting of wire, whether from the coil or when removing excess wire ends, should be carried out with jewelry wire cutters.

Cutting wire

For any jeweler, wire cutters are useful, and for those who work in wire, they are vital. There is a range of wire cutters to choose from, each with specific uses, and the best ones do tend to cost more. Poorer-quality, cheap versions are often not designed for jewelry work, and tend to give an ugly, unprofessional finish to the wire ends, ruining the piece as a whole.

Flush cutters: Used to cut wire as flush as possible with a surface. They are quite accurate and should only be used for gold, silver, copper, or brass wire. For steel wires, such as tiger tail or memory wire, you will need to use a much tougher cutter. Flush cutters cut at a slight angle and are highly accurate. They also tend to be relatively fine and sharp, allowing access to difficult or small areas. These cutters were used throughout the techniques and projects in this book.

Bevel cutters: These cut at an angle, and are not as accurate as flush cutters. They tend to be strong, so can be used for thicker and harder wires, such as steel or memory wire.

End cutters: Like bevel cutters, these are strong and are used for heavy and strong wires. End cutters cut at a straight angle perpendicular to the wire and create clean-cut edges.

Flush cutters are commonly used for wire work, as they are accurate and can access small areas easily. They are flat on one side and beveled on the other.

Bevel cutters are not quite as accurate as flush cutters, but they are stronger.

End cutters cut flat and are great for cutting the top of protruding wires as well as for cutting strong, heavy wire.

USING NYLON-COATED PLIERS

Nylon-coated pliers are useful for holding and securing wire without denting or marking it. Flat-nose versions are also good for work hardening wire. With plastic jaws, these have the strength and smoothness to allow them to be drawn along the length of wire easily. Uncoil the wire to the desired length, hold the coil with one hand, clamp down the jaws, and draw the pliers along the length of the wire. Carry out this process several times, feeling for the stiffness of the wire. Once the desired stiffness is achieved, cut the piece of wire.

HAMMERING

Hammering is a quick and easy method of tempering metal. Use a non-metal hammer such as nylon or rawhide, because metal-to-metal contact can cause marks and distortions. Uncoil the wire and put it on a metal plate. Hold the end down and tap gently with the hammer while rotating the wire back and forth. The rotating action will ensure that all sides of the wire are tempered. Move the wire along the plate and continue until the desired length is tempered. Avoid hammering close to the edge of the metal plate, as this can dent the wire.

USING FLUSH CUTTERS

When you have measured the desired length of wire, take hold of the wire at the cutting point and hold one side with your thumb and fourth finger. Using your index and middle finger, hold the other side of the cutting point.

1. Bring the wire cutters to the cutting point and position the flat side toward the reel end of the wire. Hold both sides of the wire firmly with your fingers, and use your opposite hand to squeeze the wire cutter handles firmly together.

2. The length of wire and the remaining coil are cut and secured. This method of holding ensures that no parts shoot off dangerously. The wire end attached to the coil will have a flat end, and the other will be a pinched, sharp edge. The flat end of the pliers can be applied to cut the beveled edge to give a flush, clean edge before work begins.

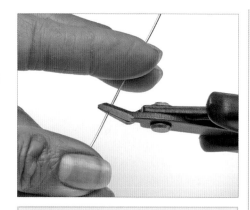

Tip: When cutting wire ends, always secure the part being removed. Small pieces of wire tend to fly away very quickly from the cutters and can easily spring into your face or even your eye. Wearing protective glasses is a good precaution to prevent injury.

CUTTING TINY PARTS

1. Hold the piece and position the flush cutters where you want to make the cut.

2. Place a finger over the end to be cut to keep it from flying away. To prevent injury when guarding the wire end, ensure that the cutting edge of the cutter is not in contact with your finger.

Tip: Always cut wire on an end of a finished piece with the flat edge of the cutters. This will ensure the ends are as finished and neat as possible, and there is less chance of sharp edges remaining.

Rounding off wire

When wire is cut using wire cutters, regardless of whether the end is flat or pinched, it can have sharp edges. In order to make it safe and neat to wear, it is vital to round off the sharp edges, especially if the wire is to be inserted into the ear for earring hoops or studs.

USING A WIRE CUP BURR

1. Cup burrs are cup-shaped files with internal teeth designed to deburr and remove sharp edges on wire ends. They are available in many sizes and in handheld or machine-operated versions, and are perfect for removing sharp wire ends. Secure a length of wire in the palm of your hand with a short length protruding from between your thumb and forefinger.

2. Hold the burr tool with your dominant hand, insert the wire into the cup end, and twist the burr wire back and forth in a rotating fashion. Remove the wire to check it with your fingers. Continue until you have a smooth edge.

FILING WIRE

1. Grip the length of wire in the palm of your hand and secure the end with your thumb and forefinger. Stabilize your hand against a solid surface, ideally the edge of a desk.

2. Take the file, emery board, or sharpening stone and file it across the edges from the bottom, moving the file with an upward action. Keep turning the wire while doing this to round off all the edges and ensure that the end does not become overfiled on one side.

Using pliers

Pliers allow you to create freeform shapes—they can bend, turn, and hold pieces, so are ideal for making wire jewelry. This section shows the properties and capabilities of various types of pliers, and introduces basic wire-forming techniques.

Regardless of the type of jewelry—beaded, wire, or fine jewelry—pliers are essential tools. They are easy to use and can grip, secure, manipulate, and shape wires into endless constructions, configurations, and bend types. As well as shaping wires, pliers are essential for connecting parts and findings and straightening wire pieces.

Pliers are available with various jaw shapes. When wire winding, the final shape of the wire is defined by the shape of the jaws—for example, round jaws will create rounded shapes. When using pliers, consider how the movement of both hands can assist in the shaping of the piece.

As well as choosing good-quality pliers (see pages 19–20) you must take care to prevent any marks or damage to the jaws—any dents or imperfections left on the jaws will be replicated on the metal being worked on.

HOW TO HOLD PLIERS

Before starting to work with wire, you should become comfortable with the tools you will need to work it, in particular pliers.

To hold the pliers, grip them with your writing hand and hold the wire with your other hand. If the pliers have a spring mechanism, hold the top arm with your thumb and grip the other side with four fingers. However, if the pliers do not have a spring action, use your index and middle finger to pull the pliers closed and your fourth and fifth fingers to push open the jaws of the pliers.

Hand-forming

Pliers not only hold and move wire themselves, but can also be used to secure the wire while you shape and form the wire around the pliers' jaws with your hands.

GRIPPING AND MOVING

Hold the wire by placing the pliers' jaws around the desired area, then squeeze the handles together to clamp the piece in place. Continue to hold the jaws down with your dominant hand to secure the wire. The jaws should always be positioned as close to the area of work as possible for accuracy.

Grip and move: Hold down the handles to secure the wire end. Clutch the remaining length of wire in the palm of your hand; the end nearest the jaws should be supported with your thumb and index finger. The pliers can now be moved forward, backward, and rotated to any angle.

Grip and manipulate: Clamp the wire securely in the pliers' jaws and use your opposite hand to guide and shape the wire around the jaws. Pliers and fingers can be moved together to create the desired shape or form.

Tip: Think about the size of the pliers you plan to use. Using too large a pair of pliers for fine wire work can be impractical and may damage the piece.

STRAIGHTENING WIRE

In addition to shaping wire, pliers can be useful for removing unwanted kinks and crinkles. To do so, it is best to use flat, parallel, or nylon-coated pliers on the problem area. Work along the length, starting at one end. Clamp onto a problem area and squeeze shut, or open and close the jaws along the length to press out the kinks. While straightening, also rotate the wire so all angles are evenly corrected. Nylon-coated pliers can be pulled along the length of wire.

GRIPPING AND TWISTING

Pliers not only wind wire and form shapes, but can also be used to move wire sections to different positions. While holding one section of a piece, pliers can be applied to another area to alter the relative angle and position.

1. Hold the piece securely by clamping down with the thumb against the fore and middle fingers. Do not secure the area intended for realignment; this should be protruding from the hand to allow access for the pliers to grip.

2. Grasp and secure the extended part with flat-nose pliers and rotate forward while moving your opposite hand, which is securing the body of the piece. Stop when the two parts are perpendicular to each other.

3. By applying this simple twist you have transformed the piece, making it more three-dimensional and placing the two end loops at different angles.

Using round-nose pliers

Round-nose pliers have tapering, cone-shaped jaws that are ideal for creating wire loops and forming rounded curves. These pliers are very commonly used in jewelry making, particularly for wire work.

CREATING CURVES

As the jaws of the round-nose pliers are cone-shaped and tapered, varying sizes of curves and loops can be created by simply aligning the wire at different positions along the jaws. Place the wire at the tip for smaller diameters; to achieve larger curves, start farther down.

Creating shapes with pliers often requires the relocation of the jaws throughout the manipulation process. For example, you can make a loop over round-nose pliers by making a semicircle before repositioning the jaws to complete the full circle. This process allows the wire to fully form around the curves of the pliers' jaws and produces a perfectly round loop.

MAKING ARCHES

In order to fashion arches in a piece of wire, the pliers need to be repositioned often and at the same jaw position. The following sequence indicates how repositioning continuously along the length of a piece of wire can create a uniform curved pattern.

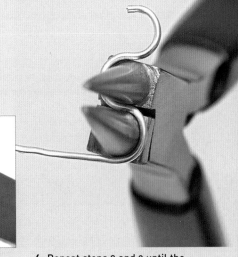

1. Grip one end of the wire and move the pliers forward until the wire is sitting at the base of the jaws, opposite the wire end. Release the piece.

2. Reposition the jaws of the pliers so the semicircle is held by the top jaw. Taking the wire end with your fingers, bend it around the bottom jaw until the wire points to the right (horizontal).

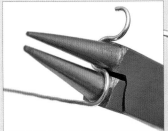

3. Loosen the jaws and again reposition, keeping them in a vertical plane; move the previously made curve into the top jaw. Bend the wire to the left-hand side across the bottom jaw. A uniform curved pattern is beginning to form.

4. Repeat steps 2 and 3 until the desired length of curved wire is achieved. To ensure that the curves are identical in size and shape, always reposition at the same jaw location. Guarantee accurate relocation by marking the pliers' jaws with a marker pen.

MAKING COILS

The shape of the round-nose pliers, although tapered, means that they are well suited to making straight wire coils.

1. Position the wire end at the appropriate position for the size of coil you want. Rotate the jaws forward, release, and continue to move forward until a full circular loop is created.

2. Guide the length of wire below the loop and continue to rotate the pliers forward while winding the wire. Release the jaws and reposition, and continue to wind forward until another full coil is achieved.

3. Continue to wrap the wire around the jaws, opening the pliers and repositioning the wire as necessary. Always wrap around at the same jaw position, pushing the coil up along the tip of the jaws to achieve a straight coil.

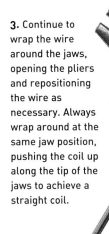

MAKING AN OPEN-ENDED WIRE LOOP

Creating wire loops is an essential technique for jewelry making. Loops can be used as a design feature on the end of a wire to keep beads from falling off, to link up to other parts, or as a point to suspend other components from. Knowing how to make a perfect circular loop will enable you to produce pieces finished to an excellent standard.

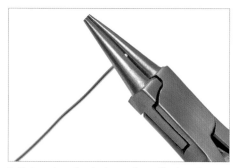

1. Take a length of wire and use flush cutters to give a flush edge to the end. Insert the end of the wire into the jaws of the round-nose pliers at a position where the desired size of loop will result. Do not allow the wire to stick out from the end of the pliers—it should lie flush with the jaws.

2. Grip the wire firmly in the jaws of the pliers, then rotate the pliers forward while using your thumb to hold the other end of the wire. Once you have a semicircle, open the jaws to release the piece.

MAKING A CLOSED-ENDED LOOP

Open-ended loops are quick to make and offer some security, but a closed-ended loop will be much more robust.

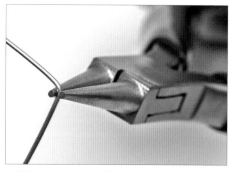

1. Take round-nose pliers and bend a right angle approximately 1½ in. (40 mm) from the end of a 4 in. (100 mm) length of 20-gauge (0.8 mm) round wire.

3. Keep hold of the wire with your hand and rotate the open pliers backward to the position where the wire is straight. Clamp down the pliers and move forward again, gripping and pulling the wire around the curve of the jaws until the two wire ends meet and a round loop is created.

4. Remove the wire from the pliers to reveal a reverse P-shaped wire piece. Hold the straight end of the wire with your fingers, and with fine chain- or round-nose pliers clamp on the inside of where the wire ends meet. Make a sideways bend so the wire end sits vertically in the center. If necessary, use flat- or chain-nose pliers in a forward-and-backward motion to bring the ends flush with each other to complete a perfect loop.

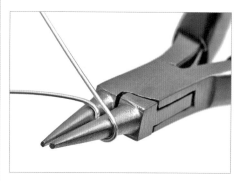

2. Move the pliers so the bottom jaw is sitting in the right-angled corner, then wrap the wire around the top jaw to create a loop.

Finished piece

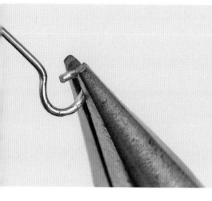

OPENING AND CLOSING A LOOP

To link a loop to another loop or component, the ring must be opened. Don't try to do this by prizing the ends apart. Instead, hold the two ends with pliers and use a forward-and-backward movement to ensure the piece is opened and closed without distorting its shape.

Forming with flat-nose and chain-nose pliers

Although they are mostly used to hold, twist, and pull wire, flat- and chain-nose pliers can also be used to shape and form it. By using these sharp-cornered jaws, you can form more angular shapes.

1. Insert the wire end into the jaws of the pliers. The end of the wire should be flush with the end of the jaws. Hold tight and use your fingers to pull and guide the other end downward across the base of the jaws.

Tip: To achieve identically sized formed pieces, mark the jaw area with marker pen where the original piece (that you want to replicate) was formed. This guideline can be followed for future pieces, and once complete can be removed with a small quantity of acetone.

3. Hold the loop end with flat- or chain-nose pliers. Using fingers or chain-nose pliers, move the wire end from the vertical position to horizontal, perpendicular to the longer length.

2. Remove the wire from the jaws and reinsert it so the length of wire after the bend is in the pliers. Taking the end of the wire, repeat the process by guiding it down along the side of the jaws. Continue until you have created a square.

4. With your fingers or round-nose pliers, grip the longer wire end and wind it forward around the wire below the loop. Wind around twice until you have created two perfect new coils below the loop.

5. Use cutters to remove excess wire, with the flat end facing toward the piece. Apply chain-nose pliers to the end, squeezing to ensure the wire end is tucked away neatly to keep it from catching.

To make a zigzag, grip the wire in the jaws of the pliers and rotate them while guiding the wire with your fingers. Once an angle has been created, reposition the pliers along the wire. Repeat until a zigzag pattern is produced.

Creating wire findings

Pieces of jewelry are often made with a combination of metal and non-metal components and findings. To join and finish the piece, findings will likely be required to link the components together and create secure fastenings that allow the piece to be worn.

Although there is an abundance of findings available to buy, handmade versions are simple to make and will ultimately coordinate with and enhance bespoke jewelry pieces. Furthermore, when making a piece of jewelry, there is nothing more frustrating than being unable to complete it due to a lack of matching findings. By having a good selection of wires and the knowledge to produce findings, you will ensure a coherent finished piece that can be made entirely by hand. Handmade findings can be as simple or as elaborate as you choose.

Some findings can be premade and stored safely for future projects; jump rings, for example, can be made in advance in several sizes, wire gauges, and colors before being stored, ready to use. However, findings such as clasps and earring fittings should be fashioned as and when required so they are consistent with the design of the finished piece.

Head pins

A head pin is a length of wire with one end that is larger or wider; this keeps a bead that has been threaded onto it from falling off. There are many types of head pin

designs, but they all share this key feature. The remaining length of wire is then twisted or wound to secure the bead in place, or linked up to another piece.

There are various lengths and gauges of head pins available in flat or beaded versions that you can buy from jewelry suppliers. However, if you make your own, you can make them to any length or gauge.

Whether it is handmade or store-bought, the length of the head pin must be straight—any kinks in the wire will keep beads from threading onto it and sitting straight. There must be enough length for the depth of the stones, beads, or other components that it is to hold, and to allow for excess wire to wrap into a loop or link to other parts.

SIMPLE LOOP-END AND CLOSED LOOP-END HEAD PINS

Use the techniques shown on pages 32–33 to make a simple or closed loop at the end of a length of wire—this will produce an eye pin. The simple, unclosed loop option is not as strong but will allow beads to sit flush with the base of the loop. The closed option is much more secure, but the bead will sit two coils from the base of the loop.

Tip: When using any piece of wire to hold a bead in place, always use the thickest that can be passed through the hole; this will give the finished piece added strength and security.

KNOTTED-END HEAD PINS

1. Take a length of wire approximately 3½ in. (90 mm) long; coil it around the top of the round-nose pliers to make two small coils.

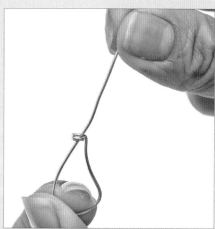

3. Curl the length of wire upward into a U-shape before threading and pulling the end through the coil from below. Continue to pull the wire, using your thumb in the curve as a lever to guide the wire upward and avoid kinks. Pull tightly with your hand or with chain-nose pliers, pulling and holding the top below the knot with nylon-jaw pliers to avoid marking the piece.

Finished piece

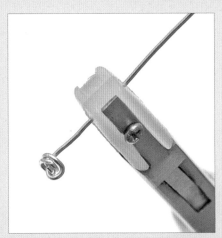

2. Continue holding the coil in the jaws of the pliers and pull the end of the wire upward so it is parallel with the pliers' jaws.

4. Once the wire has been successfully pulled and knotted, use nylon-coated pliers to remove any kinks and straighten the wire. Cut to the desired length with wire cutters, making sure the flat end of the knot is facing toward the wire end.

Finished piece

SPIRAL-ENDED HEAD PINS

1. Cut a 3½ in. (90 mm) length of 20-gauge (0.8 mm) round wire. Create a small loop at the end of the wire using the top end of a pair of fine round-nose pliers.

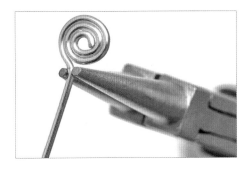

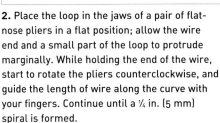

2. Place the loop in the jaws of a pair of flat-nose pliers in a flat position; allow the wire end and a small part of the loop to protrude marginally. While holding the end of the wire, start to rotate the pliers counterclockwise, and guide the length of wire along the curve with your fingers. Continue until a ¼ in. (5 mm) spiral is formed.

3. Leave the spiral as it is or adjust with pliers so the middle of the spiral sits central to the wire end. To achieve this, position fine round-nose pliers at the end of the spiral, then bend the wire to the right into a straight position.

FLATTENED-END HEAD PINS

Spreading the end of a piece of wire will keep threaded beads from falling off.

1. Lay a length of wire along a flat metal plate. With the flat end of a planishing hammer, start tapping approximately ½ in. (15 mm) from the wire end. Tap along the ½ in. (15 mm) length, then flip the wire over and repeat, so the metal on both sides is evenly spread.

2. Repeat the hammering until the end of the wire has spread out enough to keep a bead from falling off. Be careful to maintain the depth of metal and avoid overhammering, as this will thin the metal excessively, causing it to become too brittle or sharp-edged.

Jump rings

Jump rings are round wire hoops that have an opening to allow them to connect with each other and link together components or findings. They are often used in jewelry making and are essential in the making of non-soldered wire jewelry. Multiple jump rings linked together can create extremely strong and durable chain or chain mail.

Jump rings are available in almost any size, metal type, and color, but if you choose to make your own, the process of making a number of jump rings is quick and simple and requires few tools. Making your own means you don't end up with many more jump rings than you actually need, as they tend to be sold in large quantities. Jump rings can be made in advance in a range of sizes and colors, and can be stored in containers for future use. It is surprising how many you will use when making wire jewelry.

Caution: Please note that the blade of a jewelry saw is extremely sharp, so take care when sawing the coils.

MAKING JUMP RINGS

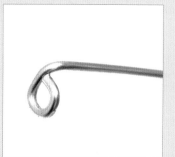

1. Unreel a length of wire measuring approximately 1½ in. (40 mm), but don't cut it from the wire reel. Loop the end and bend it with chain-nose pliers so the loop lies perpendicular to the remaining length.

2. Insert the loop into the chuck of a hand drill, pushing gently to ensure it is touching the base. Insert a drill bit (the same size as you want the inside diameter of the finished jump rings to be) and push it in as far as possible, securing the loop in place with the wire protruding from the drill bit. Tighten the chuck to hold the wire and the drill bit in place.

3. Secure the hand drill in a vise with the handle facing upward. Wind the drill handle with one hand while guiding and feeding the wire coil along the drill bit with the other. A coil of wire will start to form. Continue winding, making sure to pull the wire slightly to the right to bring the wire as close as possible to the previous coil.

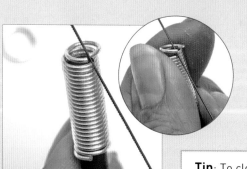

4. Cut the wire from the reel with wire cutters, remove the coiled piece, keeping it on the drill bit, and use a jewelry saw to cut a straight line down the coils. As each coil is cut, an opened jump ring will be produced. Jump rings can be cut using wire cutters, but this method will leave a pinched, sharp edge on one of the ends that will have to be cut away afterward.

Tip: To close jump rings, twist two pairs of pliers with forward-and-backward actions to maintain the round shape. Never attempt to close the jump rings by pushing the two ends together, as this will distort the shape.

Perfectly round jump rings produced from a coiled wire. These rings can be stored in a container ready for use in their open state. Open jump rings are much easier to use during linking; simply close them as you go.

Split rings

Split rings are double coils of wire that are used to connect components. To link the split ring, one end is gently levered open and a joining piece is threaded through until it becomes located in the center of the ring. Jewelry split rings are much stronger and more durable than jump rings. The opening in the split ring cannot open like a jump ring and, because of this, once attached, the piece will be very secure. Split rings are therefore ideal for joining parts that are exposed to strain, such as bracelets or necklaces, and are also perfect for connecting parts such as clasps.

Although split rings are readily available, making them by hand is simple and quick and will allow you to create any gauge, color, or size of split ring. You only need wire cutters and round-nose pliers to make them.

MAKING SPLIT RINGS

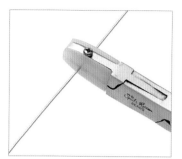

1. Temper a ¼–½ in. (70–80 mm) length from the coil with nylon-coated flat-nose pliers. Work the pliers across the length many times to achieve a ridged feel, which will ensure any formation created will remain solid and strong, with spring-like qualities.

2. Insert the wire end into the jaws of round-nose pliers, making sure the end does not point out the end of the jaws. Grip and secure the wire end in place.

3. Rotate forward and reposition the pliers when necessary to create a fully round coil. Pull the wire end around the coil and below the original wire end. Continue to rotate the pliers while winding the wire end under the original coil until a second coil is formed. To ensure that both coils are the same size, also wind the second coil in the same position as the first, pushing the first coil upward in order to create the second. Repeat to create a third coil.

4. Remove the triple coil from the pliers and cut the wire end with the flat end of the wire cutters toward the coil. Now cut the first wire end so it sits at the same vertical position as the other wire end.

5. To open the ring, insert a narrow tool—such as split-ring tweezers or pliers, or even fingernails. Regardless of the tool, take care not to pull the end outward too much, as it can stretch the coils apart. Pull only slightly to allow space for a piece for connection. Once the piece is located, remove the tool and thread the piece along the wire until it is sits securely in the center.

Should the coils in a split ring become pulled apart, put it into the jaws of round-nose pliers at an angle and squeeze the pliers. This will force the coils back together; if necessary, straighten the two coils by using the tip of the round-nose pliers.

Wire hooks

Wire hooks are really useful in jewelry, as they can be used to close a necklace or bracelet, be linked to create chain, be used as earring hooks, or simply be used for aesthetic effect. The design possibilities of hooks are endless; however, do remember that they are primarily functional, and you will need to consider carefully the length and curvature of the hook. Additionally, note that earring wires must be made from round wire; any other profile would cause discomfort to the ear.

SIMPLE S-HOOK

1. Take a 2¾ in. (70 mm) length of 20-gauge (0.8 mm) wire and use round-nose pliers to create a small looped end. Move the pliers to a position below the loop, placing the wire farther down the jaws. Guide and wrap the wire around the jaws in an opposite direction from the loop.

2. With the top half of the S-hook formed, move the pliers to below the loop before bringing the end of the wire upward around the top jaw of the pliers. Reposition the jaws if necessary to allow the wire end to curve right around.

3. Finish the piece by creating a matching small loop at the other end. Cut away any excess wire with wire cutters, with the flat end facing toward the piece. Reshape and work harden if necessary with flat-nose or nylon-coated pliers.

CLOSED-ENDED HOOK

This is a practical clasp for bracelets or necklaces and offers extra security for heavier pieces. This sequence demonstrates how to make the hook part of a hook-and-eye clasp. To create the eye end of this clasp, follow the steps shown on page 46.

1. Bend a 4 in. (10 cm) length of 20-gauge (0.8 mm) wire at the 1½ in. (40 mm) point, initially with your fingers, then put it onto a non-slip surface such as a towel. Grasp and squeeze the U-bend with flat-nose pliers. The pressure from the pliers will bring the two ends together so the wires are tightly parallel.

2. With round-nose pliers, create a loop at the bent U-shaped end. Use the tip of the jaws so the loop is as small as possible.

4. Cut the shorter length of wire, stopping approximately ⅛ in. (3 mm) from the top of the looped end. Cut with the flat end of the cutters facing toward the piece so the end is neat and flush.

5. Trim the longer length to approximately 1½ in. (40 mm), and create a loop with the wire end perpendicular to the main body of the hook.

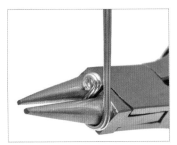

3. Move the pliers into position below the loop, using the larger part of the jaws. Pull the double wires over the base of the jaws and upward in order to create the hook part.

6. Wrap the longer wire around the loop and the ⅛ in. (3 mm) end. If this hook is to be joined to another link or part, ensure it is left open and is only closed after it has been linked. Cut any excess wire with wire cutters, with the flat side facing the piece.

EARRING HOOKS

The function of an earring hook is to fasten an earring onto the wearer's pierced ears. The earring hook, regardless of the other design features, must be longer and curved outward at the back to keep it from falling out, and must include a loop from which the main body of the earring can be suspended. With these features in mind, any design can be constructed.

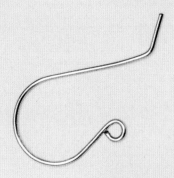

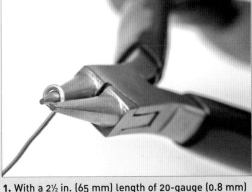

1. With a 2½ in. (65 mm) length of 20-gauge (0.8 mm) wire, create a ¼ in. (5 mm) diameter loop end. The size of the loop is dependent on the number of parts it will hold; however, bear in mind that only a certain amount of weight can be comfortably suspended from the wearer's ear. A larger jump ring can be added if necessary for linking more parts.

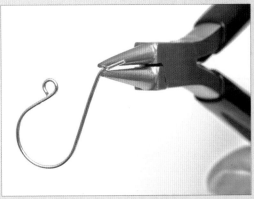

2. Shape the body of the hoop by placing it around a cylindrical rod; this can be the end of a ring mandrel or any stable and firm rod of the right shape and size. Curve from one end and then bring the end of the wire outward so it forms a slight S-shape.

3. Straighten and work harden the wire with nylon-coated pliers. Use a cup burr to round off the wire end and remove sharp edges (see page 28). This will make the wire safe to pass through the ear. Approximately ¼ in. (5 mm) from the end, bend the wire outward with round-nose pliers. During wear, the body of the earring will naturally pull the hook forward. This curve will keep the hook from falling out of the wearer's ear.

ANGULAR EARRING HOOKS

As well as curved hooks, angular designs can also be created.

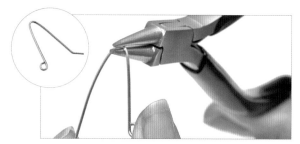

Loop the end of a 2¾ in. (70 mm) length of 20-gauge (0.8 mm) wire and make a bend at the ¾ in. (20 mm) position. A simple V-shaped hook can be created by holding the pliers at the ¾ in. (20 mm) position and then pulling the two wire ends downward. Complete by flicking the back of the wire outward using round-nose pliers.

To achieve a more angular-shaped wire hook, shape a 2¾ in. (70 mm) length of 20-gauge (0.8 mm) round wire around flat-nose pliers.

Tip: Earring wire should ideally be no thicker than 20-gauge (0.8 mm) to allow for comfortable wear.

Earring studs

An earring stud is simply a wire post with a wider or angled end that is perpendicular to the wire. This keeps the wire post from falling through the piercing in the ear. Earring studs can be created with or without loops—the addition of loops allows parts such as beads or other wire components to be suspended from them.

As with any metal that is threaded through the ear, the ends of the wire must be smooth. The wire should ideally be 20-gauge (0.8 mm)—no thicker—and the length approximately ½ in. (12 mm), to allow for a butterfly fitting to be secured. Bear in mind that a wire stud end must be large enough not to go through the pierced ear and should sit perpendicular to the wire, allowing it to be flush as possible against the ear.

Shown here are three simple stud earrings shaped from wire. To recreate all three, use around a 2¼ in. (60 mm) length of 20-gauge (0.8 mm) wire for each, cutting off any excess afterward.

LOOP-ENDED STUDS

1. Create a small loop at one end of the wire using round-nose pliers. Place the loop into flat-nose pliers and bring the wire end downward to create a right angle.

2. Cut the excess with the flat side of the wire cutter facing toward the loop. Round off the edges so the wire can sit safely and comfortably on the wearer.

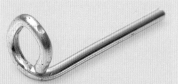

3. Repeat steps 1 and 2 to complete a pair. Butterfly earring backs are used to keep the stud secure on the wearer.

TRIANGULAR STUDS

With chain- or fine flat-nose pliers, form a small triangular shape, and then bend it perpendicular to the wire end. Repeat to create a matching second stud, and use butterfly earring backs to secure to the wearer.

SWIRL-ENDED STUDS

1. Create a small loop and then place inside flat- or chain-nose pliers to wind the wire around it in a swirl shape. Once the desired size of swirl is achieved, bend the wire end downward into a right angle.

2. Cut the excess so the remaining wire is approximately ½ in. (12 mm) long. Round off the edges. Repeat to create a matching pair of studs.

SWIRL STUDS WITH LOOPED ENDS

Adding a loop end to any stud will allow another component, be it a bead or a wire feature, to be connected and suspended.

1. Using round- or chain-nose pliers, make a right angle approximately ¾ in. (20 mm) from the wire end.

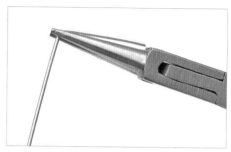

2. Place the right angle into the top part of the jaws of round-nose pliers. The shorter wire end (¾ in./20 mm) should sit flush with and parallel to the jaws of the pliers.

3. Grip the pliers' jaws tightly to secure the wire before rotating the pliers forward to create a small loop at the right angle.

4. Place the loop in the jaws of flat- or chain-nose pliers and start to guide the wire end around to create a swirl. Continue until the desired swirl size is achieved.

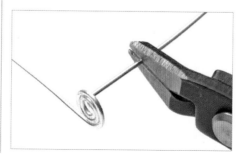

5. Cut excess wire from the shorter length protruding from the back of the swirl. Round off the end edges; this will now become the stud post that threads through the ear.

Continues on next page

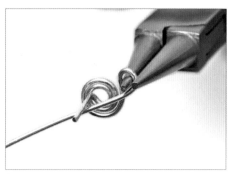

6. Use round-nose pliers to create a small loop in the remaining wire end.

7. Using a wire cutter, with the flat end toward the piece, remove the excess wire. Reshape if necessary with chain-nose pliers, making sure the wire end sits perpendicular and is straight against the back of the swirl.

The earring stud is ready to be worn, or beads and other components can be suspended from the loop. This method locates the wire in the center, allowing the stud to sit centrally against the ear.

End caps

End caps are used to secure cord, hide unsightly wire ends, or gather and cover multiple strands. Made without hoops, end caps can be fitted over a piece before a finished loop secures the piece in place. Additionally, a loop can be added to the cap end to allow it to be linked to further components. By hand making end caps you can choose the size, wire type, and gauge to suit your needs exactly.

SIMPLE END CAPS

1. Begin by making a loop on the jaws of round-nose pliers before continuing to wrap the wire, making sure the wire is wrapped below the original loop. Continue winding and rotating the pliers, positioning each newly wrapped coil around the same jaw position while allowing the previous coil to move upward; this ensures the same diameter throughout the length.

2. Once the desired length of coil is achieved, cut the wire end. The length of the cap end is dependent on the thickness of the cord/leather and the weight of the overall piece it will be secured to.

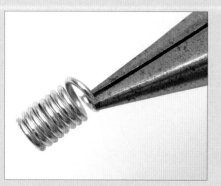

A simple end cap can secure and hide the end of a cord.

3. Using chain-nose pliers, carefully bring the top coil upward; this loop is employed to join the cap to other components. If you intend to secure the cord, put the cap onto the cord end and squeeze the coils to maintain a strong grip. Additionally, epoxy glue can be applied to further secure the fixing.

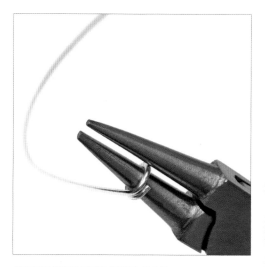

CONE-SHAPED END CAP

1. To create this shape of cap end, unlike the straight version, wrap the wire above the initial loop. Continue to follow the shape of the round-nose-pliers' jaw until the wire reaches the jaw ends.

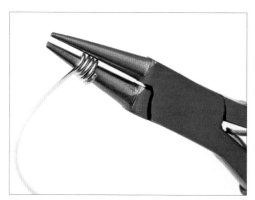

2. Cut off the excess wire. This cone can be strategically placed to cover wire parts on the ends of necklace or bracelet pieces.

Finished piece

CLOSED-ENDED CAPS

A closed-ended cap conceals more, keeping unsightly parts well hidden. This type of cap provides a more professional finish, and the central opening in the swirl gives easy access for wire to secure the piece in place.

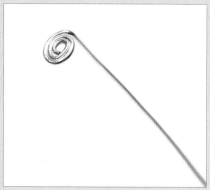

1. Following the instructions for steps 1 and 2 of making a spiral-ended head pin on page 35, create a small ⅛ in. (4 mm) diameter swirl at the end of a length of wire. Bend the wire end so it is perpendicular to the swirl.

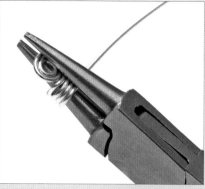

2. Hold the swirl piece between the jaws of round-nose pliers. Start to coil the end by wrapping the wire underneath the swirl and rotating the pliers. Continue until you have a length of coil.

3. Use chain-nose pliers to hold and fold the swirl piece over the top of the coil to close it off. Use pliers to neaten the parts before inserting the cap over the desired area.

Gain a professional, finished look with a closed-ended cap.

Brooch pins

Commercial brooch fittings are not overly attractive or interesting. Often the options available offer very few creative possibilities, and are usually attached and hidden behind the brooch design. With handmade fittings, all shapes and sizes can be produced, and simple or elaborate creations are both easily achievable. A handmade pin can also be incorporated into the design and worked around the piece rather than becoming a hidden finding.

Creating wire brooch fittings is simple. By twisting and shaping wire, a handmade pin alone can become a finished brooch. Additionally, beads or stones can be added, or wire features applied to decorate the piece.

A brooch fitting must have two key elements to allow it to function: One is the spring action, and the second is the sharp end, which will allow it to pierce through clothing. In order to make one end sharp, the wire has to be hammered and filed. Hammering the wire will make the metal stretch, taper, and work harden simultaneously, and will give the additional resilience required to make the brooch work.

Before you start work on a brooch pin, think about the wire gauge. The wire for a pin must be thick and strong enough to secure it to an item of clothing.

Note: A pin protector can be used at the sharp end to prevent any injury to the wearer.

MAKING A BROOCH PIN

1. Straighten and temper an 8½ in. (22 cm) length of 16-gauge (1.2 mm) round copper wire with nylon-coated flat pliers. Place the top end of the wire on a flat metal stake and tap with a planishing hammer. Hammer a ½ in. (15 mm) area from the end. While hammering, continue to rotate the wire so all angles become flattened, tapering the wire end.

2. With a flat emery stick, file in a forward movement, guiding from ½ in. (15 mm) to the wire end. File the end to a sharp point. Finish by using a very fine emery paper, which will ensure that the point is smooth and allow it to pierce through items of clothing.

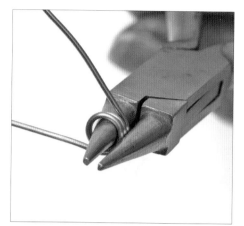

3. Measure approximately 2¼ in. (60 mm) from the pin end and coil the wire around itself twice using round-nose pliers. This double-coil feature will create the spring tension of the pin.

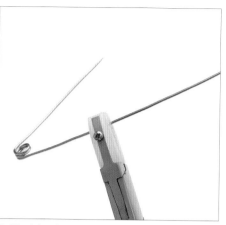

4. Work harden the piece as much as possible by running the nylon-coated flat pliers along the length of the wire on both sides of the double coil.

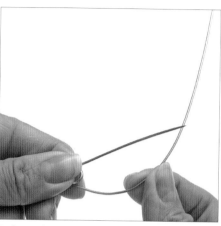

5. Curve the longer length in a "U" shape below the pin-ended wire. Do this freehand, or shape it around a bangle mandrel with a nylon-head hammer. This will temper the metal further.

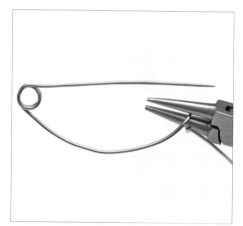

6. Create a loop end on the remaining wire length, approximately ⅜ in. (10 mm) from the sharp pin end. Use round-nose pliers and guide the wire backward and forward to form the loop. This will become the catch to house the pin.

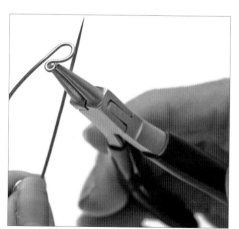

7. Cut off any excess wire, with the flat edge facing toward the piece. Leave approximately ½ in. (15 mm) and loop the end with round-nose pliers to complete the brooch-pin fitting.

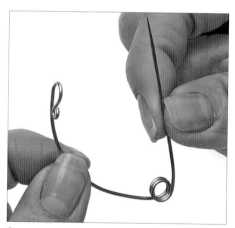

8. Pull the two wire pieces apart to create further tension and resistance between the two. When the sharp end is inserted into the curved connector it will naturally spring outward, securing the pin end into the catch.

Wire clasps

A clasp joins the two ends of a jewelry piece, allowing it to be secured to the wearer.

Machine-manufactured clasps can be technically advanced and impossible to replicate by hand, and although many types of commercial clasps are available, there are often occasions when only a handmade clasp will match and finish a piece off perfectly.

Wire-constructed clasps must have the strength to withstand stretching and pulling, so bear this in mind when selecting the gauge of wire.

HOOK-AND-EYE CLASPS

This sequence demonstrates how to make the eye part of a hook-and-eye clasp. To create the hook end of this clasp, follow the steps shown in the hook section on page 38.

1. Create a loop from a 4 in. (10 cm) length of 20-gauge (0.8 mm) round wire, ¾ in. (20 mm) from the end. The loop should be ¼ in. (5 mm) in diameter, so use the pliers' jaws accordingly, depending on the size of the pliers—a good location is at the lower-jaw point.

2. Remove the loop from the round-nose pliers and straighten the two wire ends at the center point of the round loop with chain-nose pliers.

3. Bend the longer length at the location of the short wire end so it sits horizontally, pointing toward the left side.

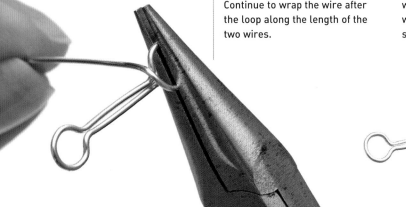

4. Create a larger loop with the longer length, and close it by winding the wire around the end. Continue to wrap the wire after the loop along the length of the two wires.

5. Wrap the wire until it reaches the smaller original loop before cutting the remaining excess wire with wire cutters. Squeeze the wire end with chain-nose pliers to secure it in place.

6. The finished eye clasp end will fit well with the previously made hook on pages 38–39. Both parts can be secured to a necklace or bracelet by the free loop on either end.

TOGGLE-AND-RING CLASPS

The toggle-and-ring clasp, like the hook-and-eye clasp, is a two-part closure and can be used for bracelets or necklaces. Additionally, if applied to the front of a neckpiece, it can produce a lariat-type mechanism. Although it offers a secure fastening, the toggle-and-ring can be more difficult to fasten than the hook clasp—however, the toggle-and-ring offers a more stylish and contemporary look.

1. Straighten and temper a length of 20-gauge (0.8 mm) wire from the coil. Cut 2 in. (50 mm), and, using round-nose pliers, bend the wire around the top of the jaws to create a double coil in the center.

2. Create small loops at both ends with the tip of the round-nose pliers. The T-bar is now complete and can be joined from the double coil to a necklace or bracelet.

3. Shape a 5 in. (12 cm) length of 20-gauge (0.8 mm) wire around a ¼ in. (8 mm) diameter rod. By gripping each wire end with chain-nose pliers at the center, straighten both wire ends so they sit flat and parallel to each other.

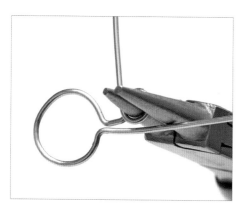

4. With the tip of the chain-nose pliers, hold one of the wires and bend it at a right angle. Position round-nose pliers above the right angle and create a round loop.

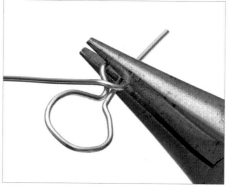

5. Wrap the wire from the end of the loop around the other wire piece twice. Cut off the excess wrapped wire and bend the remaining excess wire to form a right angle, before cutting as close as possible with the flat side of cutters. Squeeze any protruding wire ends with chain-nose pliers.

This toggle-and-ring clasp is complete and is ready to be connected to a necklace or bracelet.

Creating components freehand

Creating wire components freehand, using only pliers and wire cutters, is a practical, effective, and quick technique. It is not restrictive and gives you creative freedom to explore and develop the wire while avoiding the constraints of the set-up processes required when working with tools or jigs.

By shaping and forming components freehand, changes can be easily applied as necessary during the wire-creation stage, allowing a much more fluid form of design. This means you can be less inhibited and restrained, and you can develop a style that is not dependent on a particular tool or piece of equipment, avoiding the pre-designing "pen to paper" stage. Some outstanding designs can be created using this practical method of freehand wire work.

Freehand wire forming requires very few tools—just a selection of pliers, wires, and a pair of wire cutters. Because wire is so flexible, much of the shaping can be carried out with your fingers. Freehand wire forming can offer infinite design possibilities; this section will outline some of the basic shapes, formed links, and knots achievable by simply using pliers, cutters, and fingers. By learning the key wire-forming methods to create common shapes, links, and components, you will be able to develop quite elaborate and individual designs and concepts.

Wire links

Wire links are shaped elements created to connect one component to another, be it an additional wire part or a jewelry finding. The use of pliers to create wire links freehand allows the production of many parts very quickly, which can be further connected to form a unit within a completed jewelry piece.

During the production of a wire link element, think about how it will connect to another part, be it an open- or closed-loop ending, and allow sufficient wire to create the connection feature.

The ends of the wire sit on the sides of the trefoil shape, so the opening is hidden. Also, the completely enclosed top loop ensures that the connection to another component will be strong.

TREFOIL SHAPE

The trefoil shape is a common pattern applied in wire jewelry pieces. This double-ended style can be produced in any length and the end loops made in various sizes. The triple loop ends lend themselves to various connection possibilities that can allow the part to become a jewelry component.

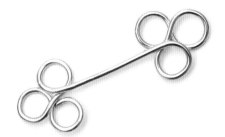

1. Cut a 4 in. (10 cm) length of 20-gauge (0.8 mm) round wire and place the end midway along the length of the jaws of a pair of round-nose pliers. Make a loop by wrapping the wire around the top jaw of the pliers. Release the loop and reposition it so the end of the loop is placed between the jaws of the pliers.

2. With your fingers, bring the remaining length of wire around the bottom jaw, wrapping it all the way around. Once the wire can reach no farther around the jaw, release the piece.

3. Place the second loop against the upper jaw and bring the wire all the way around the top. A "figure-eight" piece is formed.

4. Rotate the figure-eight shape counterclockwise so the free loop sits to the right-hand side. Wrap the wire end around the bottom jaw, bringing it all the way around until it can no longer pass the jaws.

5. Remove the piece from the pliers and position the last loop against the top jaw. Pull the wire downward around the jaw as far as possible. A perfect final loop will be formed.

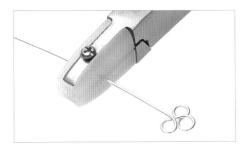

6. Straighten and work harden the remaining length of wire with nylon-coated flat-nose pliers before repeating the loop-forming process at the other end of the wire.

MULTI-LOOP HANGING COMPONENT

This technique illustrates the methods used to create a matching mirror-image component that allows connections with multiple parts. The addition of the top double-loop feature permits the piece to be attached and suspended. As larger loops are needed for this piece, the base of the plier jaws is used.

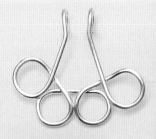

1. Take a 4½ in. (11 cm) length of 20-gauge (0.8 mm) round wire and make a loop at the midpoint, then release the piece. Leave a ¹⁄₃₂ in. (1 mm) gap before repositioning the jaws to the left-hand side of the first loop.

2. Wind the wire around the pliers' jaw to create a second loop of the same size to the left-hand side of the original loop.

3. Repeat the process on the opposite side, creating two matching loops using the wire end of the right-hand side. Now the two double loops mirror each other. If necessary, straighten and shape with fingers and pliers.

4. Flatten, neaten, and temper the piece with flat nylon-coated pliers. Once the piece is uniform, use fingers to move the two wires so they taper and meet. Using the upper end of the plier jaws, create a loop on both ends by gripping and rotating backward to create two reverse "P"-shaped loops, with the flat side facing front.

5. Complete the piece by using chain-nose pliers to flatten and bring together the two looped ends. This piece is now ready to be linked and suspended from another part. Additionally, further components can be hung from the four loops.

WAVY CURVED LINK

Many types of wavy shapes can be made with round-nose pliers, and by using square-profile wire you can create a much sharper finish with cleaner edges. Often a very different aesthetic can be achieved by simply using a different shape or gauge of wire.

LOOPED ABSTRACT HEART

Hearts are popular shaped symbols commonly applied to jewelry. This wire piece is an abstract heart shape, which is easily connected. The use of pink-colored wire adds a pop of color and also works in line with the "love" theme of a heart. Again, this illustrates how the look of a piece can be altered by applying a different color as well as gauge or profile of wire.

1. Start with 8 in. (20 cm) of 20-gauge (0.8 mm) square wire and create a small looped end using the upper part of the pliers' jaws. Bend the wire to the right around the jaws of the pliers ¼ in. (5 mm) below the loop and create a right-angle bend.

2. Move the pliers along the length of the wire approximately ¾ in. (20 mm), and hold the jaws down before bending the wire upward. Each of these bends creates a "U"-shaped curve.

1. Cut a 3 in. (80 mm) length of 20-gauge (0.8 mm) round, pink-colored craft (or copper) wire. Using round-nose pliers, carefully and gently so as to avoid damaging the pink-colored coating, create a small loop at both ends.

2. Place the wire piece into the base of the plier jaws, approximately 1 in. (25 mm) from the right-hand loop. Holding the wire securely, bend both ends upward with your fingers. A "V" shape is created.

3. Continue moving the pliers and shaping the wire along the length, ensuring that each reposition on the plier jaws is in the same position as the previously shaped curve. This will create curves in a straight path on both sides.

4. The last "U"-shaped bend will be shorter, matching the opposite end. Create a loop end to finish the piece. Reshape if necessary with fingers and round-nose pliers before hammering lightly with a rawhide or nylon-coated hammer against a metal plate to temper and retain the shape.

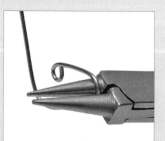

3. With both wire ends upward in a "V" shape, place round-nose pliers at the midpoint (eyeball this or measure the halfway point) of the right-hand wire. Bend the wire inward toward the "V" shape of the piece.

4. Repeat the process with the opposite wire end and shape with your fingers until you have an abstract heart shape. Once the shape has been completed, flatten and temper it with nylon-coated pliers.

SWIRL-SHAPED LINK

Fabricated wire swirls make interesting patterns for jewelry, and the addition of a loop will allow them to be securely attached and suspended.

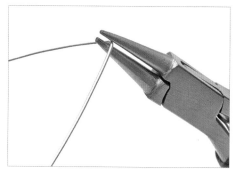

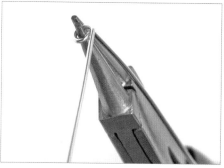

1. Take a 6½ in. (16 cm) length of 20-gauge (0.8 mm) round wire, and position round-nose pliers 1½ in. (40 mm) from one end. Bend it with your fingers to create a right angle. Release the pliers and the piece.

2. Reposition the wire piece and place it against the tip of the plier jaws with the right angle held in place. The longer end will protrude from the jaws, while the shorter wire end will be sitting flush with and parallel to the jaws.

3. Rotate the pliers with a counterclockwise movement while using your fingers to guide the wire around the curve of the jaw to make a small loop.

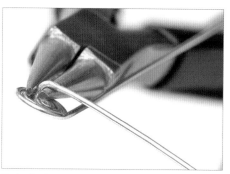

4. Place the loop into chain-nose pliers and start to curve the longer wire end around the loop to create a swirl pattern. Continue until you have a swirl with a diameter of just over ¼ in. (6 mm).

5. At the back of the swirl, create a right angle approximately ¹⁄₁₆ in. (2 mm) from the base. Reposition the round pliers above the bend, create a round loop, and close by winding the end of the wire.

6. Cut away excess wire and squeeze the end with chain-nose pliers. Straighten and temper the remaining length of the wire with nylon-coated flat-nose pliers. Beads can be inserted and the end looped to secure them. This piece can now be linked and suspended using the loop at the back of the swirl.

SQUARE-SHAPED COMPONENT

The sharp-cornered jaws of flat- and chain-nose pliers can create much more angular bends. The angled jaws of these fine and accurate flat-nose pliers are able to produce the exact and neat corners of this square-shaped piece.

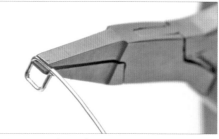

1. Cut a 4 in. (10 cm) length of 20-gauge (0.8 mm) square wire. Grip with the tip of the chain-nose pliers and bend at right angles at three equally spaced locations until a small ⅛ in. (3 mm) square frame is created.

2. Move and position the pliers' jaws ¼ in. (5 mm) from the base of the square frame before bending another 90-degree angle so the wire is sitting parallel to the opposite side of the square frame.

TRIANGULAR-SHAPED COMPONENT

This piece is produced using similar methods as for the square-shaped component, but with more sharply angled bends. To create these bends, finer sharp-cornered pliers are required; chain-nose versions are ideal.

1. Using 4¾ in. (12 cm) of 20-gauge (0.8 mm) round wire, create a triangular-shaped loop with chain-nose pliers. Bend it at ⅛ in. (3 mm) intervals, at approximately 60-degree angles, to produce the triangle frame.

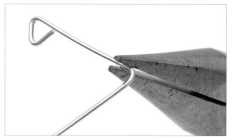

2. Measure ½ in. (15 mm) from the end of the triangle and reposition the pliers using the upper part of the jaws to grip and secure the wire. Bend the wire at 60 degrees toward the main triangle.

TRIANGULAR CLOSED-FRAME LINK

Any shaped frame, either curved or angular, can be created freehand with pliers and closed with the wire-winding technique shown to produce a shaped link. This allows the piece to be connected or suspended. Using colored wire can give the piece more definition and highlight its angular character.

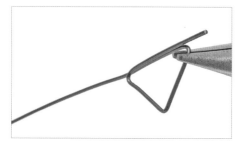

1. Using a 5½ in. (14 cm) length of 20-gauge (0.8 mm) round gunmetal wire and round- or chain-nose pliers, bend at 1½ in. (35 mm), 2 in. (50 mm), and 2½ in. (65 mm) to create this triangle shape.

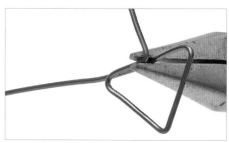

2. With the tip of the chain-nose pliers positioned slightly off-center, bend the first wire at a right angle. Repeat the process on the longer wire end, and the two should meet in the center at a vertical position.

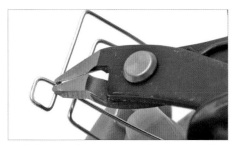

3. Measure ⅜ in. (10 mm) along, reposition the pliers, and make another right-angle bend, again following the original square frame.

4. Continue bending along the length of the wire to create an open square coil. Bear in mind that with each outer square the length increases before a right-angle bend is made; this ensures that each square is larger than the previous one.

5. Finish the wire end by creating a square link that matches the size of the original. Cut and remove any excess metal. The piece can now be attached or suspended from the top square loop.

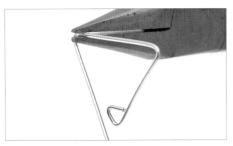

3. Continue to bend the wire at 60-degree angles to create a complete triangle frame. Make one final bend so the wire end is horizontal.

4. Measure ½ in. (12 mm) from the left-hand angle and bend at a right angle so the wire is vertical. Shape the wire to make a downward-facing triangle; this will enable the component to be attached to a chain.

5. With the wire end, wrap around the base of the triangle to close it. Cut off excess wire with wire cutters and squeeze the end with chain-nose pliers to prevent protrusion.

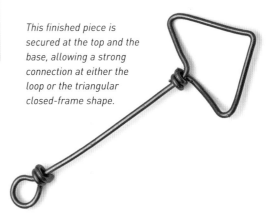

This finished piece is secured at the top and the base, allowing a strong connection at either the loop or the triangular closed-frame shape.

3. Insert the triangle shape into the jaws of nylon-coated flat-nose pliers and secure in place. Taking the shorter wire end, either with fingers or with round-nose pliers, wind the end around the longer length at the base of the triangle. Remove any excess wire with cutters.

4. Create a loop at the end of the longer wire and close securely by winding the wire end back around. Cut off the excess with wire cutters and squeeze the end with chain-nose pliers.

Wire knots

Wire knots make interesting and attractive jewelry features, and can become the key element in a piece or an essential component of a design. Knots are strong both aesthetically and physically, and can turn a simple piece of jewelry into a unique and eye-catching creation.

Often in jewelry making, lengths of cord, leather, or yarn can be bound and knotted in various ways to secure metal components or jewelry to the wearer. Using knotting methods with wire creates charming components that can be joined, linked, or suspended in various ways to complete a jewelry piece.

Metal wire is much more difficult to tie than cord or material, and wire knots will likely be looser than those tied in yarn. Take care to avoid pulling the wire too tightly or quickly, as this could kink or dent it.

TRADITIONAL KNOT

1. Shape a 4 in. (10 cm) length of 20-gauge (0.8 mm) round wire into a circular shape. This can be done freehand, or on a ring mandrel or round rod. Cross over the two wire ends until a ring shape with a diameter of approximately ¾ in. (20 mm) is formed.

2. Guide the wire end that is sitting at the front of the circular shape to the back, and then bring it through the center. Squeeze the piece gently together with your fingers to decrease the size of the knot, and at the same time pull the two wire ends gently downward.

3. Shape the wire freehand with your fingers and flat- or chain-nose pliers. Once an even knot shape is achieved using the nylon-coated flat pliers, squeeze it flat and work harden the piece.

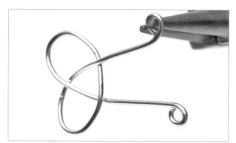

4. Complete the piece by using the tip of the round-nose pliers to create loops on both wire ends. Reshape by hand or with ring-nose pliers if necessary, before work hardening the piece with nylon-coated flat-nose pliers.

LOVERS' KNOT

This knot is comprised of two knots bound together.

1. Cut two 3 in. (75 mm) lengths of 20-gauge (0.8 mm) round wire and make a knot with one piece. Adjust and straighten the wire ends so both sit on a horizontal plane.

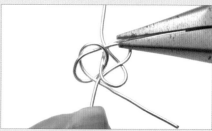

3. The two knots are now connected. Adjust and shape them with the help of chain- and ring-nose pliers, as well as your fingers. Take time to manipulate the knots so they become uniform and match as much as possible.

5. Use round-nose pliers to create loops at all four wire ends. Once this is completed they can be connected at any of the four loops.

REEF KNOT

This knot is simple to make and is ideal for bangles or rings.

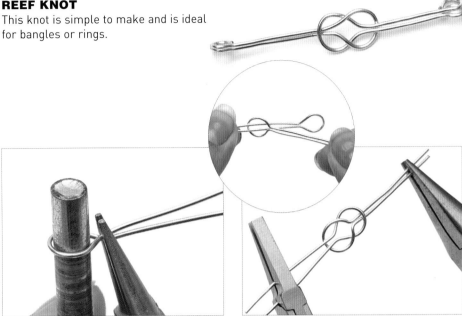

2. Thread the second length of wire through the base of the first knot in the center. Once the wire has been threaded through halfway, tie a knot.

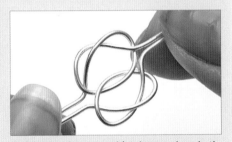

4. Once you have matching knots, place both flat into nylon-jaw pliers; this will flatten the two knots. At the same time, use your fingers or chain-nose pliers to straighten the four wire ends so these sit parallel to and aligned with each other.

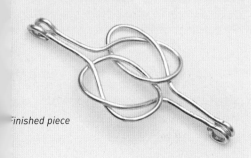

Finished piece

1. Cut two 3 in. (75 mm) lengths of 20-gauge (0.8 mm) round wire and wrap each around a ¼ in. (7 mm) rod to create two loops. Bring the two wire ends together by pinching them together in the center with round-nose pliers while each is wrapped around the rod.

2. Insert the double wire ends of each piece into the loop of the other piece, bending the wire ends slightly if necessary. Once both are inserted, straighten the loop and wire before grabbing both double wire ends and pulling them in opposite directions.

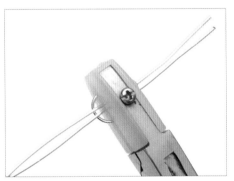

3. Place the double inserted pieces into flat nylon-coated pliers and squeeze them tightly together. This action will allow the two parts to become more entwined and flush together.

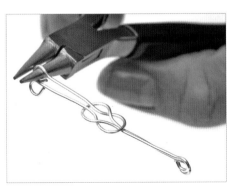

4. With round-nose pliers, finish the piece by creating loops at the four wire ends. Neaten and temper as necessary with the nylon-coated flat pliers.

FIGURE-EIGHT KNOT

This type of knot is ideal for a centerpiece, or a number of small versions can be created to make an interesting chain.

1. Cut a 5½ in. (14 cm) length of 20-gauge (0.8 mm) round wire. At 2 in. (50 mm) along, bend it around the top of a standard ring mandrel. Pull both sides so the wires cross over each other to form a uniform circle. Remove from the ring mandrel.

2. Position the loop above the ring mandrel and, taking the longer wire end, wrap it around and upward to the top of the mandrel to create a figure-eight shape. Remove from the mandrel.

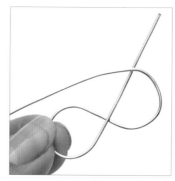

3. Taking the straight-ended wire, thread it under the opposite curved, longer piece of wire and pull it through the other side.

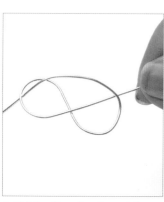

4. Holding the wire piece at the base of the right-hand-side loop, guide the longer wire into the original left-hand-side loop. Thread through and pull the wire under the loop.

5. Place ring-nose pliers with the curve on the inside of the left loop and pull the top wire end to neaten and tighten the loop. Repeat this process on the opposite loop, pulling on the lower wire end to neaten the figure eight.

Loops can be formed on the two wire ends so the piece can be joined to other parts and components.

CELTIC KNOT

There are many types of Celtic knots; the one shown here is a simple and commonly used version.

1. Take an 8 in. (20 cm) length of round 20-gauge (0.8 mm) wire from the coil, but do not straighten it; allow it to keep its natural wound shape. Using the tip of the round-nose pliers, grip 2½ in. (65 mm) from one end and bend the wire.

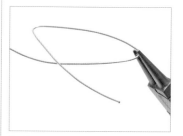

2. Measure along the length again and make another bend 2 in. (50 mm) farther along from the original bend. Bend inward, and the two wire ends should cross over each other.

3. Use your fingers to shape the piece so it becomes domed at the top. This shape will make it easier and allow the longer length of wire to be guided and threaded through to the back.

4. Pull on both wire ends to create a "three-petal" shape. Shape with your fingers to ensure all three shapes are even in size and length—approximately 1 in. (25 mm).

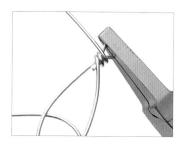

5. Create a loop with the shorter length of wire and, using the longer length, wind and secure it closed. Reshape if necessary until the three petal shapes are evenly shaped and spaced out.

This finished knot can be linked from the top loop or from any of the three petal shapes.

BOWS

Bows are pretty and fun features, which when made in wire are ideal for applying to rings, earrings, necklaces, or bracelets; the possibilities are endless.

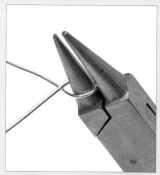

1. Take a 5½ in. (12 cm) length of 20-gauge (0.8 mm) round wire. Wrap at 2 in. (50 mm) around the jaws of round-nose pliers until the two ends of the wire cross over and meet at a point.

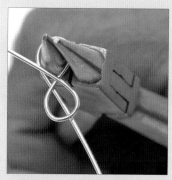

2. Remove from the pliers and reposition the jaws to where the wires cross over. Take the slightly longer length of wire and wrap it around the jaws until the wires cross over. A figure eight is formed.

3. Hold the left-hand-side loop with fingers or chain-nose pliers and take the longer length of wire; wrap it around the midpoint twice. Leave the length of wire at the back of the figure eight.

4. Reshape using your fingers and round-nose pliers until the two sides of the bow are matching and the two wire ends are tapering away from each other. If you like, squeeze the two bow shapes smaller with flat-nose pliers.

5. Check that the two wire ends are equal in length and cut away any excess if necessary before using round-nose pliers to create small loops at both ends. This piece is now complete and can be suspended directly from a chain.

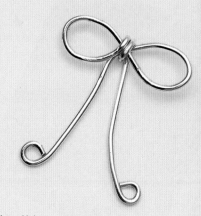

Note: Using angular pliers such as chain- or flat-nose pliers will produce more angular and square-looking bow shapes. Experiment with various pliers and shapes and sizes of wire.

Once the three coils have been linked to one another, a slightly spherical shape is formed, and chain or wire can be threaded through the center to allow this shape to remain intact.

DANISH KNOT

Although it is known as a knot, this is constructed by the linking of wire coils as opposed to the tying of wire.

1. Following the instructions on page 36 for creating a jump-ring section, use a ¼ in. (5.5 mm) diameter rod to create a length of coil.

2. Count down four rings along the coil and pull slightly apart to insert cutters. With fine wire cutters, cut at the same vertical line as the top ring end, four coils down. This will produce a single coil made up of four coiled rings.

3. As the first ring on the length of coil has been pulled upward, cut half the loop away so the coil is perfectly flush with the rest of the coils. Count down four coils and again pull apart, then insert wire cutters and cut a "four-coil" piece. Repeat the process to produce one further four-coil piece, so there are three pieces in total.

4. To create the knot, all three coils must be linked together. Begin to connect two by inserting one coil into another. Use split-ring pliers or fingernails to gently pry open the coil before inserting the second coil. Rotate to thread the coils of the second piece until it is completely connected to the first.

5. Connect the third piece into the central coil; now all three coils should be joined together by the middle "original" coil. If any of the coiled parts have become pulled apart then, using round-nose pliers, insert the jaws into the coil and position at a slant before squeezing the pliers gently. This will pull the coils together without distorting the round shape.

6. With the aid of round-nose pliers and your fingers, grasp hold of two outer coils, insert one into the other, and wind the two together. This process can prove difficult; however, perseverance and time will deliver excellent results, as once the three are connected the piece becomes instantly three-dimensional.

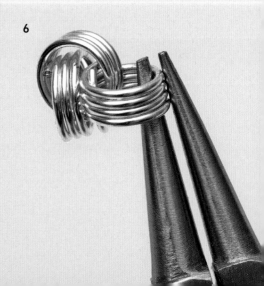

Securing beads and stones

A piece of jewelry is seldom complete without the addition of a beautiful colored stone or a selection of vibrant beads to enhance it.

Stones and beads are among the traditional non-metal embellishments used in jewelry; however, there are many other contemporary components you can use, from porcelain to Perspex, and from die-cut leather to wool, and even wood ... the list is almost endless. Regardless of the non-metal element applied, learning the basic techniques to secure these embellishments with wire will give you the freedom to experiment with your designs.

Wire is such a versatile material; it is malleable and does not need to be thick to be strong. Even the finest gauges of wire, if wound and bound correctly, will be able to hold components securely.

There are many methods of encapsulating and securing beads and stones. Often the method of securing is determined by the shape of the bead or stone, or the position of the drilled hole. This section presents some of the commonly applied techniques. Some of these can be easily modified to cater to personal taste, or to the type and shape of stone or bead. Use the following techniques as starting points, and adapt them to suit your own designs.

SIMPLE BEAD LINK

This is a simple and common technique applied to secure any shape of bead with a centrally drilled hole. The links on either side of the drilled hole can be opened to allow for linking to other parts and components.

1. Cut a 2½ in. (60 mm) length of 20-gauge (0.8 mm) round wire and create a small loop at one end. Thread on a bead and allow it to drop to the loop end. Measure ½ in. (15 mm) from the top of the bead and, using wire cutters with the flat side toward the piece, remove the wire end.

2. Grip the wire directly above the bead with the tip of the round-nose pliers and bend the wire downward to create a right angle.

3. Position the pliers at a right angle, then wrap the wire around to make a loop. Make sure you position the wire at the same place on the jaws of the pliers as before so you get a loop that is the same size. Cut away the excess wire with wire cutters and manipulate the end with chain-nose pliers until it sits flush with the loop.

CLOSED WIRE LOOP

A closed loop offers added security. This is essential when the loop is used to join jewelry pieces that will be subjected to vigorous movements and strain, such as necklaces or bracelets. Closing the loops allows the links to remain joined.

Tip: To link to another piece, both loops should remain open to allow the joining to take place before the loop is secured by winding. Alternatively, an open loop can be connected before it is securely closed or jump rings or split rings employed.

1. Take a 5½ in. (14 cm) length of 20-gauge (0.8 mm) wire and use round-nose pliers to make a right-angle bend 2½ in. (50 mm) along. Create a loop at the position of the right angle and close by wrapping around the shorter length of wire three times (see pages 32–33). Cut the excess wire away with wire cutters and squeeze the wire end with chain-nose pliers.

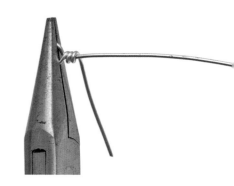

2. Thread the bead so that it sits flush against the closed loop. Position round-nose pliers above the bead, leaving a space of approximately ⅛ in. (3 mm) before making a right-angle bend.

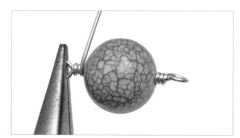

3. Create a round loop above the right angle and twist the wire around the ⅛ in. (3 mm) length below to close it off. Remove any excess wire with wire cutters, and use chain-nose pliers to secure any ends that are sticking out.

CAP END, CLOSED LOOP

Creating a cap end to a loop not only adds to the design of the piece, but prevents the wire loop from pulling through beads with large holes, while also discreetly covering any visible gaps, resulting in a more professional finish.

1. Cut a 6½ in. (16 cm) length of 20-gauge (0.8 mm) round wire and bend a right angle 2¾ in. (70 mm) from the end. Thread a bead onto the wire and push it to the right angle. Make a loop at the opposite wire end, then close by winding the wire around twice.

2. Make a closed loop on the right-angle side, and close again by winding twice. The bead is now secured in the center of the wire.

3. Take one wire end and, instead of cutting away, pull the end down toward the bead so it starts to sit flush with the top of the bead. Continue to wind until you have made a ¼ in. (7 mm) round swirl.

4. Repeat step 3 on the opposite side of the bead until you have a matching ¼ in. (7 mm) round swirl covering the hole. Remove excess wire with cutters, then use pliers to secure the wire ends on both sides by squeezing them into the swirl. If necessary, use chain-nose or flat-nose pliers to straighten both loop ends so they face the same way and are centered.

WOUND WIRE PENDANTS

1. Drop or pendant stones often have a horizontally drilled hole. To encapsulate and suspend a bead with a horizontal opening, the location of the loop and the closing varies slightly. Cut a length of round wire slightly narrower than the diameter of the drilled hole. Thread the wire through the hole and position the bead centrally on the wire before bending the two ends upward into vertical positions.

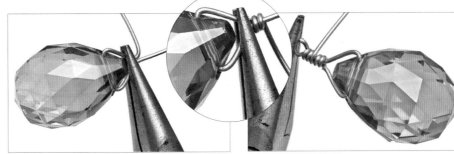

2. Hold the two wire ends with your fingers, cross them over, and with round- or chain-nose pliers pinch above the top of the bead so the wires meet. The lengths of wire above the bead should be parallel with each other.

3. With chain-nose pliers, bend one wire at a right angle and then wrap it around as close to the bead as possible, twice. Remove any excess wire with wire cutters, with the flat end facing the piece.

4. Leave a space of approximately ¹⁄₁₆ in. (2 mm) from the top of the wound wire, and with the second wire end make a right angle before making a round loop. Wind the end downward around the loop until it meets with the wound part below. Cut off any excess wire.

QUICK METHOD

1. Cut a length of square-section wire, using a gauge suitable for threading through the drilled bead. Feed the wire through the hole and place the bead in the center of the wire. With your fingers, bend the two wire ends upward into vertical positions.

2. Using round-nose pliers, grip hold of one wire end and rotate it backward to create an inverse "P"-shaped loop. Repeat the process with the remaining wire end. The angles of the loops mean the bead will be easily suspended and will sit comfortably against the wearer.

3. Pull the two loops closer together by squeezing them with your fingers at the top. Chain or links can now be threaded through and joined to both loops.

WIRE WRAPPING: BEADS

This method secures beads in fixed positions along a length of wire. The wire can then be shaped or formed further at a later stage. As illustrated earlier in the book, wire wrapping can create many shapes and sizes of coils; however, this technique of wrapping thinner wire along a heavier-gauge central wire produces a neat and intricate detail along a wire length. It offers a secure method for combining wire with wire and wire with beads, and allows you to secure many beads to wire quickly, whether to a length or to a formed wire piece.

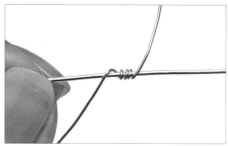

1. Cut a 16 in. (40 cm) length of 24-gauge (0.5 mm) round wire and wrap it ¾ in. (20 mm) from the end of a 4 in. (10 cm) piece of 20-gauge (0.8 mm) round wire. Wrap tightly around five times, holding the end firmly and wrapping each coil as close to the last as you can. If the coil starts to loosen, use chain-nose pliers to squeeze it together.

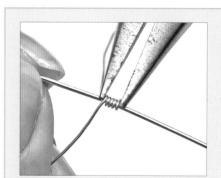

Tip: When you start wrapping, make sure you leave enough of an end to keep a hold of.

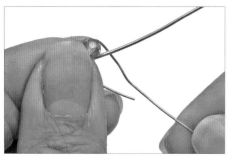

2. Thread a bead onto the thinner 24-gauge (0.5 mm) wire and pull it along to the end. Hold the bead in position with your fingers while continuing to hold the central wire in the palm of your hand.

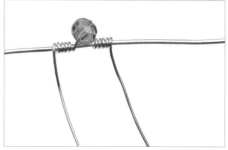

3. Pull the thinner wire from the bead and continue to wrap it around the central wire as tightly as possible. Coil the wire around five times, then thread a second bead onto the thinner wire.

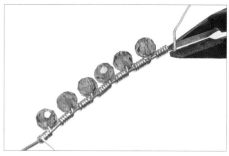

4. Continue to thread beads and wind. Repeat until the desired length is created—and once this is achieved, wind the thinner wire around the central wire five times before cutting the end with wire cutters and securing it by squeezing it with chain-nose pliers.

Tip: Beads can also be threaded onto the central wire rather than onto the thinner winding wire. Thread the bead onto the central wire, then move the thinner, wrapped wire over the top of the bead and wrap it around the central wire on the other side to secure the bead in place.

WIRE WRAPPING: CHAIN OR RHINESTONES

Lengths of rhinestone or metal chain can be secured to a central wire using the same method. This wire-wrapped piece can then be further shaped and formed.

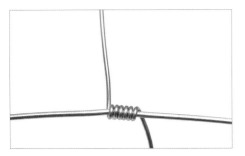

1. Just as in the previous technique, wrap thinner wire around the end of the thicker central wire five times.

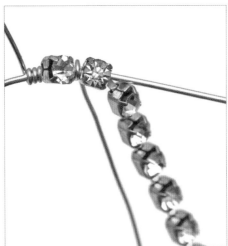

2. Hold the rhinestone chain and postion it on the central wire. Grip both with your fingers before winding the thinner wire around the space between each crystal. Wind around twice, or more if the gap is larger, then move to the next space and wrap the wire around twice (or more) again.

3. Once the rhinestone chain has been secured to the central wire, hold the joined pieces in a vertical position. This will allow the chain to fall straight so there are no kinks along the length.

4. Continue winding thinner wire along the length of the rhinestone chain until it is completely joined to the central wire. Wrap it five times around the end and cut away the excess wire, then squeeze the end with chain-nose pliers to secure.

WIRE WRAPPING: NON-DRILLED STONES

This type of stone wrapping secures non-drilled stones within shaped wire frames. The following lengths and dimensions have been specifically designed around a drop cabochon stone with dimensions of 1½ x 1¼ in. (40 x 30 mm). To estimate the length of wire required, wrap thin-gauge wire around the stone you want to use, and add approximately 2 in. (50 mm) x 2 of extra wire to create the attachment detail at the top of the wire frame above the stone.

1. Cut three 8½ in. (22 cm) lengths of 18-gauge (1 mm) round wire and straighten it using your hand and a soft cloth (see page 26). Secure the wires together with masking tape at both ends. Measure and mark the following positions with marker pen:
3–3¼ in. (75–85 mm)
4¼–4½ in. (10.5–11.5 cm)
5¼–5¾ in. (13.5–14.5 cm)

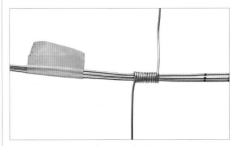

2. Wind 20-gauge (0.8 mm) wire around the three marked sections. Begin with the first section on the left-hand side, moving along and taking care to keep the three wires flat and parallel with each other.

Continues on next page

3. Position the central coiled wire section at the center of the base of the cabochon stone, and shape the bound wire pieces around the stone. Use a ring mandrel if necessary to create the curve at the base first, and then wrap around the stone.

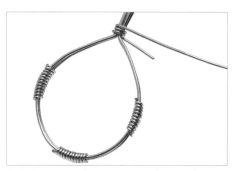

4. Bring the two bound ends at the top of the cabochon stone together with your fingers, then neaten them and bring them even closer together with flat nylon-coated pliers. Wrap 20-gauge (0.8 mm) wire around the top five times.

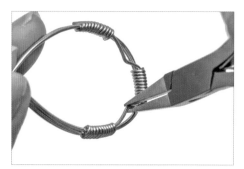

5. Insert fine flat-nose pliers at the base of the piece and grip the top wire where the base coil starts. Move the pliers' jaws clockwise inside the frame to create a right angle toward the center. Repeat this on the opposite side, moving the pliers counterclockwise, and at the wire coils on each side.

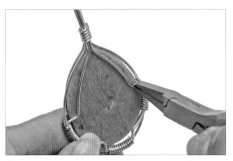

6. Insert the stone with the front facing into the cagelike frame, and press downward on the surface of the stone so that the four right-angle wire parts secure it. Flip the piece over and repeat step 5 on the new top wire to firmly hold the stone within the frame.

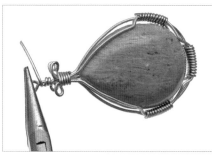

7. Once the stone is completely secured, pull the six ends apart; the central two can remain in the middle, and the outer four are cut and coiled. With the central two wires, wrap one twice around the other. Cut off the excess and then create a loop before wrapping closed with the other end.

Tip: During the wire-winding binding of the three main wires, spend time shaping the bound piece, and ensure that the three central wires remain flat and parallel with each other. Any imperfections now will affect the piece later on.

SECURING AN UNUSUAL CUT STONE

Stones come in all shapes and sizes, and securing one without a drilled hole can be a challenge. However, encasing it in a wire cage-type construction will hold it securely. When encasing an awkward-shaped stone, the idea is that the wire should fit around the stone like a glove—tight-fitting, but sufficiently loose to prevent damage to the stone. Recognize that each stone is unique, and adapt this technique to suit your particular piece.

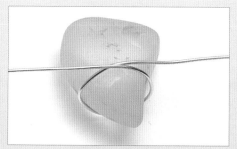

1. Always start a wire cage by wrapping wire around the narrowest part of the stone. This should become the base of the cage, so when gravity naturally pulls the stone downward it will sit securely inside the wire construction.

2. Remove the wire from the stone and wind one end of wire around the other three times to make a closed loop.

3. Put the stone back into the loop, with the wrapped part at the back. Bring the two wire ends over the top of the stone and around to the front. Pull tightly so the wires are flush against the stone.

4. Bring one of the wires under the front loop and guide it back up to the top of the stone. Pull this wire as tight as possible.

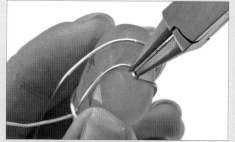

5. While pulling this wire, with one hand and using round-nose pliers, hold the wire at the top of the stone and twist it in a clockwise direction. Two curves will be formed, creating a sideways S-shape.

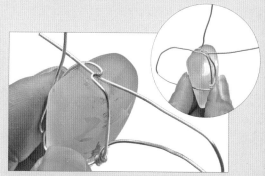

6. Guide the remaining wire length under the first curve and pull backward while bringing the other wire end forward, then thread this through the other curve. The two will cross over and hold the stone securely in place.

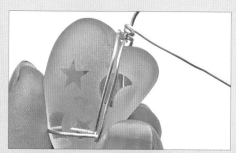

7. Take one of the crossed wires and wrap it around the other twice to secure it. Cut away any excess with wire cutters.

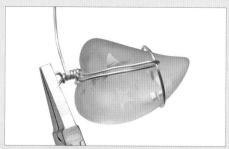

8. With the remaining length of wire, form a loop and close it by coiling the wire end around the base. Reshape and move the wires around the bead if necessary to make it as secure as possible from all angles.

Using a jig

Jewelry jigs are instrumental in creating multiple identical wire shapes easily and quickly. All kinds of wire can be applied to a jig to create any type of configuration and pattern. In this section, many shape-forming techniques are demonstrated, including some that show that the configuration of pegs does not necessarily resemble the finished shape of the wire piece. Instead, this is determined by the direction in which the wire is guided and shaped.

A wire jig is essentially a back plate with holes spread across the front face, in which various sizes of pegs can be slotted and secured. The larger the diameter of the peg, the greater the size of loop or ring that can be achieved; the smaller the peg, the tighter and smaller the loop will be. Once you have the desired configuration of pegs, wire is then shaped around them to create repeated, uniform shapes and patterns. This allows you to accurately position curves at exact locations, for example; it is ideal for creating collections of jewelry, matching sets, or chains.

There are many kinds of wire jigs available, made from metal or plastic, and with square, round, half-round, and half-square pegs. They may be small and handheld, or tabletop, hands-free, adjustable-head varieties. Additionally, there are single-use wire-forming jigs intended for small, specific wire designs or to produce jewelry findings such as earring hooks. Although there are many commercial wire jigs in various configurations available, it is also simple to create your own. By using graph paper, a piece of wood, drills, and nails or pins,

making a replica of a commercial jig is easy. Drilled holes on the wood secure and hold the nails or pins in place to shape the wire around. Alternatively, single-use jigs can be fashioned from a wooden block, nails, and wooden rods; the secured pins and rods are held permanently in place to allow for the manipulation of wire.

Unlike typical commercial jigs, permanent-pin varieties offer security without the risk of pins detaching during use, and as the pins are not removable, the jig can be preserved for future use, which allows the jeweler to create and save a library of jig patterns. If you choose to use a removable-peg jig, keep a note of the pattern or position of pegs for future reference. It is always a good idea to keep spare examples of the formed wire piece to use as a template for future pieces. By placing the sample piece on the jig, exact peg locations can be replicated. Alternatively, a photograph of the peg/pin pattern can be saved for future use.

If a piece becomes misshapen during its removal from a jig, keep the pegs in place on the board and return the piece in its original configuration so that it can be reshaped.

The basics of using a wire jig

Whatever the jig is like, the basic technique remains the same. To understand and begin to use the jig, first consider the shape and pattern you want to achieve. Record the desired pattern on paper and work from this. Recognize that pegs are placed both to allow wire to be wrapped around to replicate the peg shape, and to wrap around to locate a bend. The size of the wrapped shapes and the angles of bends are dependent on the size, shape, and location of the pegs.

Tip: If you are considering the use of precious metal wire, practice new shapes with lower-cost wire first. Once you are confident in the design and the necessary length of wire required, you can progress onto the precious wire of your choice.

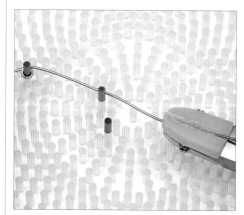

4. Cut 4 in. (10 cm) of the tempered wire, take it to the jig, and leave approximately ½–¾ in. (13–19 mm) before positioning the wire on the first peg. Hold the ½–¾ in. (13–19 mm) wire end with one hand while pulling and coiling the other end around the first peg with your fingers. Use nylon-coated pliers to offer a stronger, tighter grip if necessary.

SETTING UP

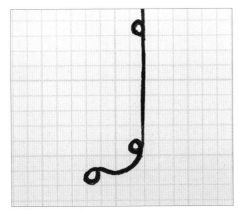

1. On a sheet of grid or graph paper, draw your design. First, sketch the desired shape, then mark the locations of pegs with circles.

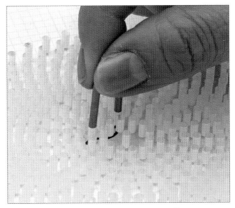

2. Once the peg sizes and number of pegs are determined, position pegs in the correct configuration by inserting them into the holes across the front face of the jig board. If the plate is made from transparent plastic, the drawing can be placed behind it as a guide for peg location; if the board is opaque, the pegs can be positioned by eye.

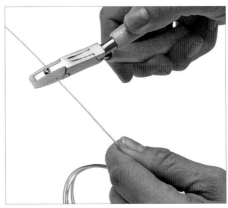

3. Take a coil of 20-gauge (0.8 mm) round copper wire and, using nylon-coated flat-nose pliers, straighten a lengthy strand while it remains in its coil. This straightening process will also temper the wire and help it retain its formed shape.

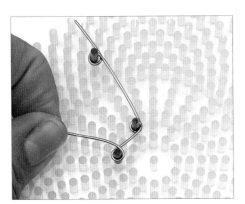

5. Continue following the configuration of the pegs, pulling the wire as tight as possible around each peg to ensure the wire in between is straight and even. Use nylon-coated pliers to pull if necessary. Use your fingers to hold the shaped wire down and prevent the piece or pegs from lifting upward out of the board.

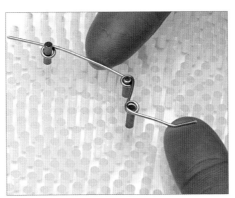

6. Once the shape is created, remove the piece from the jig by pulling gently upward with your fingers. Alternatively, the pegs can be pulled off to release the piece. While removing the piece avoid excess pulling, as this will distort the shape—although it can be reshaped, this is not ideal.

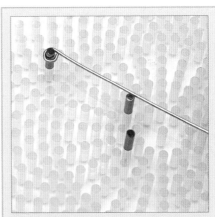

An alternative option is to create a loop at the end of the wire. Insert this loop over the first peg before wrapping and shaping begins. This loop anchors the wire to the peg, keeping it in place during the wrapping process.

Using jigs to create wire shapes

A blank paper template is often supplied with the wire jig; photocopying this will give you a supply of graph paper that matches the specific tool. Some brands also offer downloadable templates. Alternatively, you may take inspiration from the jig and pegs themselves, with designs realized spontaneously and directly on the board.

ROUND SHAPES

These can be created by wrapping wire over round pegs or around a group of pegs shaped into a curve.

1. Position the pegs to suit your design. Here, to assist in the wrapping and shaping of the two larger pegs, a smaller peg has been positioned next to the larger one as an anchor point.

2. Cut a length of tempered wire that is sufficient to wrap around the pegs, with an excess of approximately ¾ in. (20 mm) at either end. Create a small loop on the end of the wire with round-nose pliers, making sure the loop will fit over the anchor peg.

3. Wrap the loop over the anchor peg, holding it down if necessary with one hand, and use the opposite hand to grip and pull the wire. Continue to pull the wire, guiding it toward the first peg.

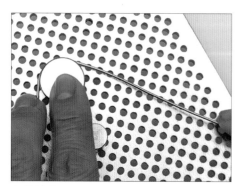

4. Hold the pegs down with your fingers while using your other hand to pull the wire around the peg as tightly as possible. If a peg is lifted up, the wire will become trapped below and the shape will distort.

5. Pull the wire entirely around the first peg and then lead it to the lower peg, guiding it around the left-hand side. Continue to pull the wire around the lower peg, bringing it around to a full circle, with the wire ending on the right side of the peg.

6. Using your fingers, lift the shaped wire gently upward from the pegs to avoid distortion. Once free from the jig, remove the extra anchor loop with wire cutters. If necessary, reshape the wire piece with ring-nose pliers or place it back over the pegs to reshape. Use nylon-coated pliers to temper and work harden the piece.

REPETITIVE SHAPED LENGTHS

Lengths of patterns or repetitive shapes are ideal components to create on a wire jig.

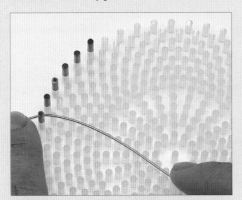

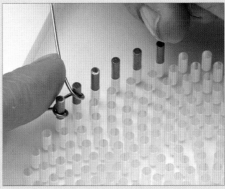

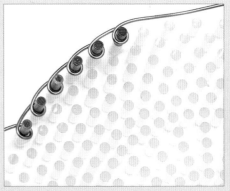

1. Insert a row of identically sized pegs along the peg board. They may be in a straight or curved line. This example has been placed along the outer edge of the peg board, which is slightly curved—the finished formed shape can always be straightened later.

2. As the pegs are very close to each other, use untempered wire to allow the wire to move around easily between them. Cut a length from the coil and leave a length of approximately 1 in. (25 mm) free at one end. Place the wire on the first peg and wrap it around in a clockwise rotation. Lead the wire onward to the next peg.

3. Holding the wire down with one hand, continue to wrap in the same clockwise direction around each peg. Always wrap in the same direction so the wire sits on the same plane, achieving a uniform pattern and side view.

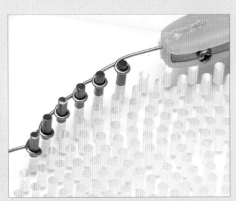

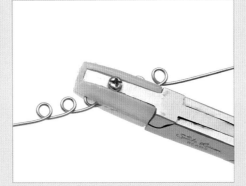

Tip: Often when the pegs are positioned very close to each other, wire is formed on one peg before the next peg is added to the board. In this way you can build up a design.

4. Once the last peg has been wrapped, use pliers to pull forcefully to ensure the wire has been shaped around the pegs tightly. Nylon-coated pliers will not mark the wire but do not offer the best grip. If there is sufficient wire to cut away the marked end, use uncoated pliers for better grip. Keep pegs from being pulled out by placing fingers over the top.

5. Remove the shaped piece from the pegs carefully and use nylon-coated pliers to flatten and neaten the piece. This will also temper the wire and help it keep its shape, as well as straightening the slightly curved angle. Due to the consistent direction of wire wrapping, the side view is also uniform.

Tip: When shaping wire around pegs, use your other hand to hold and rotate the jig base to help you guide the wire around the pegs.

ANGLED SHAPES

Some wire jigs are available with square pegs that make it easy to produce angled bends; however, these aren't essential. Careful placement of pegs will allow the wire to be shaped into angular bends. Do bear in mind that defined sharp corners are not always achievable on a wire jig; however, once the piece is removed from the jig, the corners can be emphasized using flat-nose pliers.

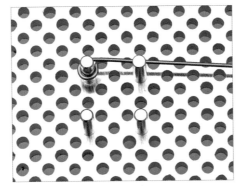

1. Position the pegs so that each represents a sharp bend—here are four pegs spaced equally to allow a square shape to be achieved. A length of wire is tempered and straightened, and a small loop is created with round-nose pliers on one end.

2. Place the loop on one of the pegs, then pull and shape the wire around the four pegs. Continue to wrap and shape the wire around the four pegs, using your fingers to pull it as tight as possible. Use pliers if necessary to pull the wire tighter and straighten it.

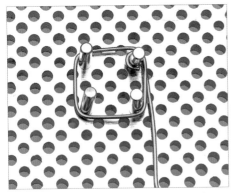

3. In addition to driving and shaping the wire, while the jig is positioned on the work surface, rotate it with the opposite hand to give a smooth wrapping action. Continue to shape and wrap wires around the pegs until the wire returns to the original peg.

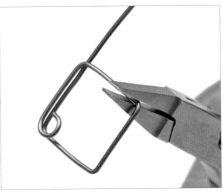

4. Insert sharp-cornered flat-nose pliers into each of the four square-shaped corners and squeeze to sharpen them. (Leave them as they are for rounded corners.) With wire cutters, remove the original loop from the inside of the square frame.

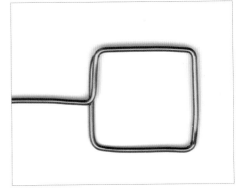

5. Insert the flat-nose pliers into the center of the wire frame, and angle the wire end upward. This piece can be further shaped with the creation of a loop or a closed loop that will allow it to be connected to other components.

ZIGZAG SHAPES

As well as using a crinkle-shape maker (see page 78), zigzag- and wavy-shaped wires can be easily replicated using a jig. Long shaped lengths are possible without lengthy peg insertions along the jig board. A short configuration can be followed with wire before the partially shaped piece is relocated along the jig so that wire shaping can continue.

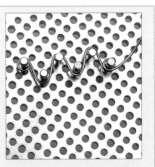

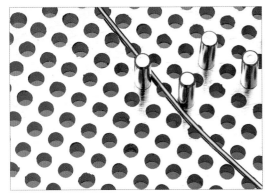

1. Place six pegs into the jig as shown, at diagonal locations. Hold a length of tempered wire at the first peg, leaving a short end of wire free. The wire should sit between the first and second pegs; this position keeps the wire from moving when the shaping begins.

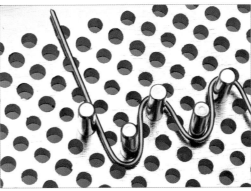

2. Hold the short end of the wire end down with one hand and use the other to pull and guide the length along the pegs. Wrap the wire under the lower and over the upper pegs, and repeat until the wire reaches the last peg; shape the wire end upward.

Tip: Again, an alternative option is to create a loop at the start of the wire so it can be placed onto the first peg before being shaped in the same method. This will create a zigzag-shaped wire piece, and a matching loop can follow at the opposite end of the wire. This shaped piece can be directly connected to further components from the end loops.

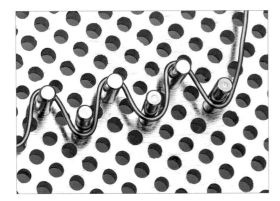

3. Lift the piece and relocate it so the end of the shaped wire now sits at the beginning of the peg configuration. Hold the shaped wire down with one hand and, using your free hand, pull the wire and continue to shape it around the six pegs. Continue this process until the desired length is achieved.

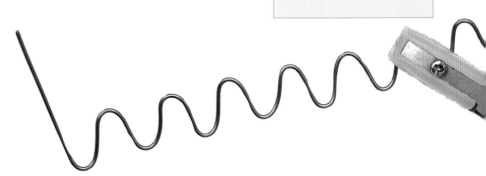

4. Once the shaped length is completed, remove the piece from the jig, reshape, and flatten with nylon-coated pliers before removing any excess wire with wire cutters. Should the piece become distorted during the shaping process, use nylon-coated flat-nose pliers to squeeze and reshape it, and also to temper it.

SYMMETRICAL WIRE COMPONENTS

In order to create a shape that is both symmetrical, you must determine the center point of the peg configuration so the start and end of the wire meet. Also, the shaping process must begin at the center of the wire, on the central peg. Finally, each wire wrap must be mirrored to ensure both sides are identical.

1. Insert pegs in a symmetrical configuration. Take a length of wire and create a loop in the center of the wire with round-nose pliers. Place the loop over the central peg.

2. Wrap the left-hand wire around the left peg and do the same for the right-hand wire. Make sure the wire is wrapped in the same direction on both; bring the wire down and wrap from the inside of each peg. Use fingers—or, for greater pull, use flat-nose pliers.

3. Continue to feed the wire ends down toward the last peg, before wrapping both ends around this final, centrally located peg. Gently remove the wire piece by lifting it upward from the pegs.

4. Straighten and flatten with nylon-coated flat-nose pliers. Use fingers or pliers to reshape if necessary.

5. Finish by winding the wire ends together. Alternatively, the ends can be removed with wire cutters to reveal the round loops, which can be used to join the piece to other components.

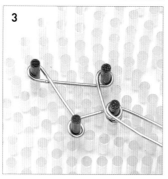

CREATING PATTERNS AND SHAPES

Part of the appeal of using a jig is the ability to create multiples of shapes. A specific peg configuration does not necessarily denote the final shape or pattern; simply changing the direction of the wire or the wrapping steps can alter the finished shape drastically. Shown here are three wire shapes created from one peg configuration.

At the design stage, determine the peg pattern. Set the pegs into the base board as desired or follow the configuration shown here. From this simple configuration, you can see that three very different wire pieces can be achieved.

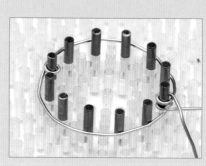

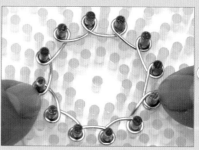

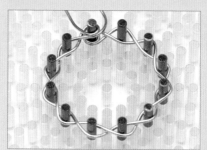

Three differently shaped wire pieces created from one jig configuration. These were achieved simply by changing the wire direction.

ADDING BEADS

It can be difficult to visualize the addition of beads onto wire while the part is being shaped and formed on a jig; however, this can be a very useful technique. Forming the wire piece and adding beads at the same time means you don't need to add them later. This can also give the piece added strength and prevent distortion.

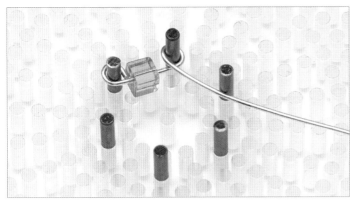

1. Insert the pegs and begin to wind wire around them. Before shaping the wire around the second peg, thread a bead onto it. Push the bead as far toward the first peg as possible. Wrap wire around the second peg; the bead is now secured.

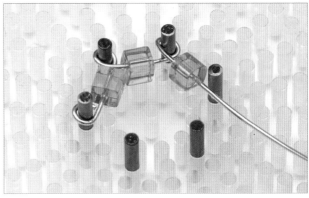

2. Continue to wrap the wire around the next peg, then thread on another bead before proceeding to wrap wire around the next peg. Each bead will be secured in place when the wire is wrapped around the following peg.

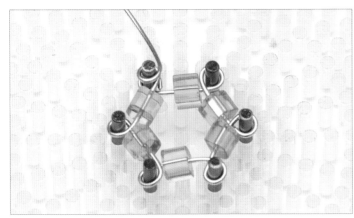

3. Repeat the process, encasing six beads in total. On reaching the first peg again, wrap the wire around to create a final loop. Lead the remaining wire end upward.

4. Carefully remove the piece from the pegs and use fine flat-nose pliers to grasp and squeeze each individual wire loop flat. This will compress and straighten the piece, as well as temper the wire to ensure it maintains its shape.

5. Use the round-nose pliers to neaten the piece and position the start and end loops so they sit on top of each other. You can connect more parts to any of the loops.

Wire coiling

There are two types of wire coiling. In the first, hand-wrapped wire is applied directly to lengths of wire. This process adds coiled features to a piece, secures parts (such as beads, chains, or numerous wires), and strengthens the area the wire is wrapped around. The second type is where wire is wrapped around a rod and, once a desired length is completed, the rod is removed to leave a hollow length of coil. Here we look at both methods.

The technique of wrapping wire to create coils produces neat and uniform lengths of joined loops. What's more, the coil can be further shaped or coiled to create detailed spiral beads that can then be linked to jewelry parts. Coiled components make interesting jewelry features that can add structure and strength, and by attaching different sizes of coiled pieces you can really elevate a simple design into an elaborate and interesting jewelry piece.

Hand wrapping wire around another piece of wire makes an interesting and detailed feature, and offers strength and stability. Hand coiling is a simple technique, but can be time consuming; however, the outcome is very worthwhile. This type of wire wrapping or coiling can be achieved on any length of wire as long as the wire being wrapped is a heavier gauge than the wire being applied. Using varying gauges, colors, shapes, and combined wires (such as pre-twisted wires) can add decorative detailing to any jewelry piece.

When numerous pieces and types are required for a particular design, a coiling tool can save time and offer uniformity. There are several tools available to buy that have similar properties, and some that offer advanced features such as the ability to create cones and other shaped, wire-coiled components. The benefit of using a coiling tool is the ease and speed with which uniform lengths of coils are achieved, and there is also the possibility of reinserting coils to produce multiple coiled and colored components.

Hand coiling

Hand coiling is a good way to learn the basics of wire winding. You can use this technique to bind and secure almost any parts together, be they stones, beads, wires, or other components. Hand coiling can be achieved across varying gauges of wire and can be applied anywhere, as long as there is a thicker core of single or multiple wires that the wrapping wire can be coiled around.

GETTING STARTED

1. Straighten a 7 in. (12 cm) length of 16-gauge (1.2 mm) round wire with nylon-coated flat pliers. Cut a 16 in. (40 cm) length of 20-gauge (0.8 mm) round wire, and use flat-nose pliers to make a bend at one end, about 1½ in. (35 mm) from the end.

2. Insert the folded thinner-gauge wire into the thicker-core wire, and hold the shorter length downward and the longer one upward. Use flat-nose pliers to squeeze the thinner-gauge wire closer to the central wire to secure it in place.

3. Hold the inner-core wire and the end of the thinner-gauge wire securely in your less dominant hand, gripping them in place with thumb and forefinger. Using your dominant hand, pull the wrapping wire forward and around the core wire. Continue to wrap the wire with a forward action, making sure that each coil sits flush with and parallel to the previous one.

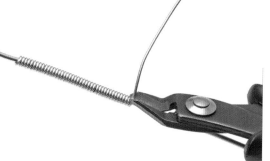

4. To ensure that the coils sit as tightly and as closely as possible to the previous coil, hold the wrapping wire about 1¼ in. (30 mm) from the area of coiling. This will allow you to grip the coiling wire and lever it forward and over the central coil easily. As the coil grows in length, move the hand that is securing it along to the end of the coil to offer as much support as possible.

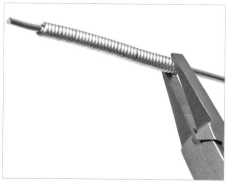

5. Once the desired length of coil is created, cut both wire ends with the flat part of the cutters facing inward toward the piece. Tuck both ends into the core wire by squeezing them with flat- or chain-nose pliers.

The finished piece can be shaped and formed or connected to other parts by creating loops on both ends.

Using a coiling tool

Coiling tools are wonderful pieces of equipment that enable you to create coils of different sizes, or to make various types of coiled beads. Unlike hand coiling, where you coil the wire onto a central core wire permanently, the coiling tool permits the wrapping of wire around a selection of internal rods. A variety of wires can be wrapped around an internal rod with a handled end, which allows you to move with greater strength and consistent rotations to create lengths of even coils. Once the desired length is created, the coil can be removed from the tool and rod to reveal a perfect coil. Here we look at creating single, double, and triple coils, and at adding beads.

SINGLE COIL

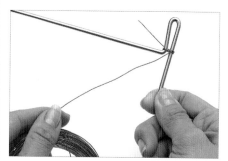

1. As lengths of coils require quite a substantial amount of wire, it is best to use the wire straight from the reel. Take the end of the wire and wrap it around the bend of the cranking rod at least three times to fasten the wire securely in place.

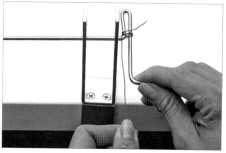

2. Secure a C-clamp to a table top and insert the cranking rod, pushing it close to the clamp but leaving a small space to fit two widths of wire. Sit at the table and place the wire reel on your lap. Pull the wire over the top of the U-bend of the cranking rod and tug firmly while using your other hand to rotate the cranking rod forward.

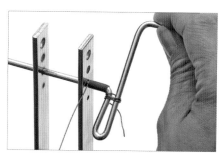

3. A coil will begin to form. Continue to rotate the crank rod forward while holding the wire and feeding it toward each new coil. Pulling the wire straight backward and feeding it toward the rod will ensure that each coil is sitting as close to the next as possible.

4. Remove the cranking rod from the C-clamp and cut the wire end with wire cutters. The length of coil can now be easily slipped off the cranking rod and threaded as a jewelry component, or further shapes can be coiled.

DOUBLE COIL

Once a length of coil has been created, it can be applied to a piece of jewelry as it is, or it can be further shaped or coiled. To coil it further produces a larger, stronger tubular bead with open-spaced coils—ideal components for bracelets, necklaces, and earrings.

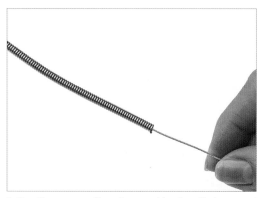

1. Use the 1.5 mm diameter cranking handle to create a 6 in. (15 cm) length of coil from 24-gauge (0.5 mm) round wire. Insert 20-gauge (0.8 mm) round wire through the length of coil and pull it through the other end.

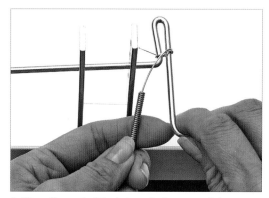

2. Wrap the end of the internal wire around the cranking rod three times to secure, and insert it into the C-clamp. Bring the length of outer coil away from the cranking rod before rotating forward to wrap the internal 20-gauge (0.8 mm) wire, until you have approximately ¼ in. (5 mm) in length.

3. Push the pre-coiled length up to the cranking rod, and start to rotate the rod forward. The length of coil will start to wind around the cranking rod. Continue to push and feed coil into the rod, allowing it to wrap around neatly.

4. Once the length of coil has been completely wrapped, guide the internal wire onto the rod until you have created a ¼ in. (5 mm) length of coil, matching the opposite end. With wire cutters, cut the length of wire from the end and then remove it from the cranking rod. The bead is complete.

TRIPLE COIL

Coiling a piece a third time produces a shorter but more voluptuous and detailed bead. The triple coil uses the previous two techniques and coils the double-coiled length to produce an even more elaborate and interesting piece. This works particularly well with contrasting darker and paler metal combinations.

WIRE COILING WITH BEADS

The addition of beads to a coiled piece adds color to all surfaces of the piece. This simple and quick technique is an extremely effective method for creating colored bead-encrusted components.

1. Insert an internal wire into the double-coiled length of wire, and secure it to the cranking rod. Pull the double-coiled part down and coil the internal wire, approximately ¼ in. (5 mm) in length.

2. Once a ¼ in. (5 mm) single-coiled length has been created, slide the double-coiled piece to the top and continue to rotate the cranking rod forward, pushing the double coil so it starts to wrap around the rod. Continue rotating the cranking rod until the end of the coil is wound completely, then guide the internal wire to create a matching length of single coil on the end.

3. Remove from the cranking rod with wire cutters and tidy up the two ends; if necessary, remove any excess coils to ensure that both sides match. This bead can now be incorporated into a jewelry piece.

1. Thread an 8 in. (20 cm) length of wire with 1/16 in. (2 mm) beads before following the previous winding techniques. Wind a few coils of the wire along the cranking rod, approximately ¼ in. (5 mm), before pushing and guiding the beads up toward the cranking rod. Rotate the rod forward to allow the beaded wire to coil around the rod.

2. Continue to rotate the rod while feeding the beaded wire, doing so gently to avoid breaking any beads. Hold the beaded wire lightly and allow it to feed naturally onto the cranking rod; do not push or stretch too tightly, as this can cause irregular coils or may cause the beads to crack.

3. When the last bead on the wire has been coiled, continue to rotate the crank rod until an extra ¼ in. (5 mm) of plain wire coil is produced. Remove the piece carefully from the rod using wire cutters.

This beaded component is now ready for use.

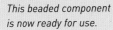

Crinkle-shape maker

Although wavy and angular shapes can be made with pliers, the crinkle-shape maker creates neat and uniform lengths of wavy or zigzag wire. This is a very simple piece of equipment that can quickly and effectively turn straight wire into uniformly shaped lengths.

Once a length of wire has been shaped, it can be formed further into rings or bangles, or lengths can be cut and manipulated into other jewelry components. Additionally, the lengths of wire can be finished with looped ends and linked with other components to produce drops for earrings, necklaces, pendants, or various other jewelry pieces.

Despite the advantages of using a crinkle-shape maker, it can only produce two different shapes, and only works with the finer gauges of wire. Heavier-gauge wire will not pull through the hole or the rotating wheels and can damage the tool; the ideal wire to use is round and no thicker than 20-gauge (0.8 mm).

Tip: It is quite useful to place a nonslip sheet underneath the tool to give it stability.

GETTING STARTED

1. Insert the two identical cogs for the design you want—the angular for zigzag wire and the round version for curved, grooved wire. The handled cog should be inserted into the right-hand side if you are right-handed, and the left-hand side if you are left-handed. Ensure the tool is placed on a nonslip surface.

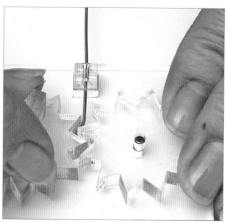

2. Cut a length of wire and insert it through the wire guide. As the wire is threaded through with one hand, push into the cogs slightly and use your free hand to turn the handled cog; the opposite cog will also begin to rotate. The wire will catch in the cogs and start to feed through. As the winding continues, the movement of both cogs will draw and shape the wire.

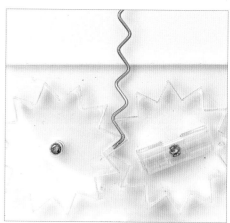

3. Continue to turn the handled cog, but at the same time hold both cogs down with your fingers. This will keep the wire and the cogs in place. For heavier-gauge wire, assist the movement of the cogs by turning the non-handled cog with your fingers. Once the length of wire has passed through the cogs, it will be released from the opposite side, and is now shaped and ready for further use. Temper if needed.

The completed piece can be shaped and formed, or loops can be created on the ends to link with other components (see page 32). Alternatively, the curved cogs can be applied to create a more rounded, wavy length of wire.

Wire spiral maker

A spiral maker, as its name suggests, makes wire spirals that are neat, uniform, and free from marks from pliers.

Although simple to use, there are limits to what is achievable with this piece of equipment; only wire that is 20-gauge (0.8 mm) and narrower can be inserted, and the largest possible size of the spiral is no larger than just under ¾ in. (18 mm) in diameter with the use of the regular-sized tool. In order to achieve larger-diameter spirals the large spiral maker must be used, which is capable of creating spirals up to 1½ in. (32 mm) in diameter.

With very little effort, perfectly shaped spirals can be formed. Also, by using a spiral maker, spirals of the same size can be replicated, allowing you to make matching pairs for earrings, or produce multiples for duplicate sets or a suite of jewelry.

The completed piece is perfectly shaped and evenly flat. The wire end can be shaped to form a loop by which the piece can be connected to others.

SETTING UP

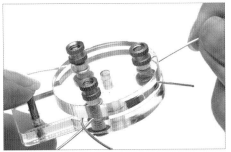

1. Loosen the three screws. Cut three 2 in. (50 mm) lengths from the same coil of wire that the spiral is to be made from. Bend each length into loose "V" shapes and insert between the clear plates beneath each screw. Bend the ends together and push them down over the side of the round plate. The wires act as dividers, keeping the plates equally separated.

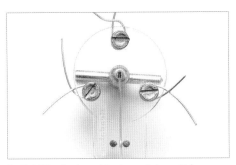

3. Hold the tool upside down; take a 10 in. (25 cm) length of 20-gauge (0.8 mm) round wire and feed one end through the two metal rods. Insert it between the two clear plates and guide it into the channel of the handle; rotate the handle if necessary. Allow the end of the wire to thread but not pass through the channel, and rotate the handle forward fractionally to hold the wire in place.

5. Remove the handle before loosening the three screws, which will allow the removal of the spiral. Pull the spiral gently by the remaining length of wire and exit through the gap between the screws.

2. Re-tighten the screws, leaving a uniform gap between the two clear plates to allow space for the wire to produce evenly flat swirls. Insert the handle via the central rod into the hole in the top plate. Note that a channel on the central rod is where the wire is threaded into and held in place.

4. Place the tool on a flat surface and use your dominant hand to rotate the handle with a clockwise action. At the same time, slightly tug at the wire so it starts to wrap around with a neat and even curve. After a couple of rotations a spiral will begin to form; continue to rotate the handle until the desired diameter of spiral is created.

Using jewelry mandrels

Mandrels are essential to the formation, shaping, and sizing of metals, particularly wire. By wrapping wire around a shaped mandrel, you can create rings, bangles, jump rings, coils, and various other forms.

Often, wire can be easily formed around common household objects: bottles, rolling pins, drills, wooden dowels, knitting needles—the list is almost endless. However, the object selected must be durable enough to withstand the winding of the wire. Wooden dowels are available in various sizes, so can be great for wrapping wire; however, if wrapped too tightly the wire can quickly become embedded in the soft wood. It is also important to be able to secure any makeshift mandrel, either by hand or in a vise, if practical.

Although household objects can be employed as a substitute, using a proper jewelry mandrel ensures accuracy and uniformity and will enable you to produce more professionally finished components and jewelry pieces—so they are well worth the investment.

Jewelry mandrels are available in wood, plastic, and steel. Wooden mandrels can work well with wire, but can be easily marked and damaged. Plastic mandrels are practical and function well for wire work; however, they are not as hard as metal versions, so thicker and harder wires will be more difficult to wind and shape, and cannot be held in vises or clamps. Steel mandrels are perfect for metalwork, especially wire; their strength, availability in various shapes and sizes, sizing guides, and hardness (which allows wire to be tempered while wrapping) make them ideal.

Mandrels are also available in various sizes and shapes: tapering cones, stepped versions, or straight lengths. Stepped mandrels are ideal for making short lengths of coils, while straight mandrels are more suited to producing longer lengths of coils with a consistent diameter, perfect for jump-ring production. During use, the mandrel must either be secured by hand or else be strong enough to be held in a tabletop vise.

USING A RING MANDREL

Although mainly used for shaping and forming rings, ring mandrels are also extremely useful for all types of curves and cylindrical forms. The following steps show how to make a cylindrical ring using the ring mandrel. Before forming the wire, measure the size required with a ring sizer. Once you know this, you can work in the correct location on the ring mandrel.

Tip: Once the wire shape has been formed, always work-harden the piece so it will retain its shape (see page 26).

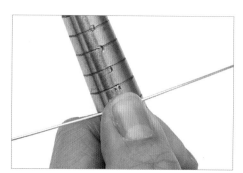

1. Take a length of wire that is longer than you need to make the ring. Hold the mandrel in the palm of your hand and place the wire across the mandrel, at five sizes smaller than the desired size. (This is appropriate for single rings or loops. For multiple coiled rings, shape at the desired size.) Once the shape has been formed, you will push it to the desired size to create a perfectly sized loop with the ends meeting. If you start shaping at the desired size, the wire ends tend to spring away from each other.

3. Wrap the length of wire around the mandrel until the wire ends cross over each other. Pull both ends so they are as tight as possible and use your fingers to shape and form the wire along the mandrel.

2. Use your thumb to bend the wire around the left-hand side of the mandrel and secure it in place. Using your other hand, pull the other end of the wire around the mandrel to the back. Use some force, stretching as tightly around the mandrel as possible.

4. Remove the formed loop and check the shape. Then place it back on the mandrel and push downward to the correct size (here, it is K). This action will open the loop up and bring it to the desired size. The excess wire can be cut away or bound together to secure the ring.

MULTIWRAPPING ON A RING MANDREL

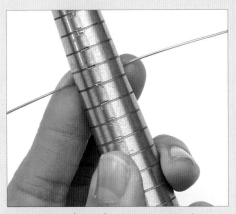

1. Cut a 24 in. (60 cm) length of round wire, then place the midpoint at the back of the ring mandrel at the desired size. Hold the wire at the back while pulling the two ends forward around the mandrel.

3. Wrap both the top and bottom wires around the mandrel twice before guiding both ends back to the top of the mandrel. You should now have a coiled ring.

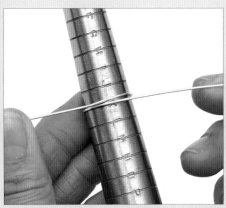

2. Pull one side of the wire over the top of the ring mandrel, then repeat with the other end underneath the first wire end and in the opposite direction. Do not cross the wire over; allow one to sit above the other on the length of the mandrel.

4. Remove the ring from the mandrel and manipulate it with your fingers to straighten and reshape it if necessary. You may need to put it back on the mandrel upside down to ensure the top and base diameters are the same. Once reshaping is complete, straighten the two ends with chain- or flat-nose pliers before crossing the two together.

Beads can be added to the wire ends before securing the two parts together. Alternatively, loops or shapes can be formed to complete the ring.

USING A BANGLE MANDREL

Almost identical to a ring mandrel, a bangle mandrel will create larger-diameter hoops that can be used for wristwear, earring hoops, or various other jewelry components. The steps described for using a ring mandrel will also work with the bangle mandrel.

In the previous demonstrations, the wire ends were finished after shaping and winding around the mandrel; however, ends can be shaped and finished even before the wire is formed around a mandrel. Demonstrated here is an adjustable bangle, which is formed around the mandrel after the wire ends have been looped. Finishing the ends first reduces the risk of the bangle becoming misshapen after forming.

Note: Bangle mandrels are also available in oval profiles, for making oval shapes.

This process can be applied to more elaborate and detailed wire ends. As shown here, the end finish would have been difficult to achieve after forming without distorting the bangle.

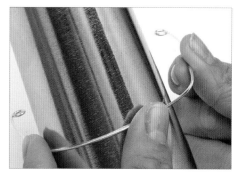

1. Secure the bangle mandrel in a vise or hold it in place with your hand. Cut a length of round wire, using the flat side of the cutters on both ends. With round-nose pliers, create loops at both ends of the wire.

2. As you did with the ring, position the wire and hold it at a size on the mandrel that is smaller than the intended size. Place a thumb over the top of the wire and hold it down around the mandrel as tightly as possible. Do the same at the other end of the wire.

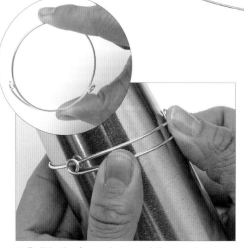

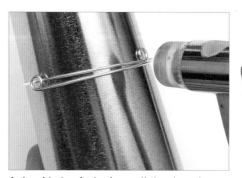

3. Pull both wire ends around the mandrel as tightly as possible while shaping them around the curved form. Then remove the piece from the mandrel and squeeze the loop to make it smaller, before putting the wire back onto the mandrel.

4. As with the single ring, pull the shaped bangle down on the mandrel to the required size. Tap it gently with a nylon-coated hammer: The hammering will ensure the wire is formed exactly to the shape of the mandrel and is tempered at the same time.

5. This piece is completed by altering the angle of the loops and threading them onto the opposite wires, locking the two together to create an adjustable bangle. Creating the loops first avoids any distortion to the shape.

USING A MULTI-MANDREL SET

This technique uses interchangeable mandrel heads with tapering steps that can be inserted into a handle.

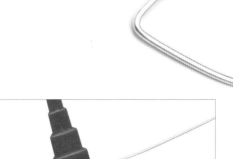

Simply by changing the shaped top, a number of different-sized circles, ovals, triangles, or square shapes can be achieved.

1. Select the desired mandrel head and insert it into the handle. (Grip the handle with your non-dominant hand.) When working with the smaller dimensions near the upper part of the head, move your grip farther up the mandrel to support the piece.

2. Select a size along the mandrel head and place a cut length of wire against the starting edge of the chosen step. Keep the wire in position with thumb and forefinger and, using the same fingers on your other hand, guide and shape the two ends around the shaped mandrel.

4. This piece can now be finished by adding beads, or by winding one end around the other. By closing the ends, this piece can be added to another jewelry piece.

3. Rotate the tool with one hand while guiding both ends of wire around the mandrel, until both cross over. Carefully remove the shaped piece from the tool and straighten with chain- or flat-nose pliers.

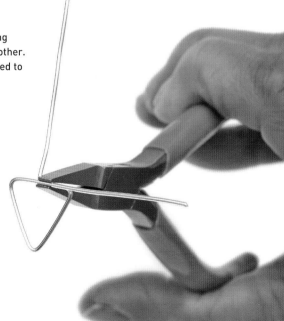

French knitting

French knitting is traditionally associated with yarn; however, wire lends itself to this technique and produces very intricate, delicate, but strong pieces. The ability to produce very long pieces that are lightweight, durable, and comfortable to wear makes French knitting a good technique for wire jewelry making.

The process of knitting wire can quickly and easily produce large pieces, or alternatively small, delicate, lacelike sections. The method of binding the wire also makes the end result strong and durable—ideal for jewelry that requires a lightweight element, such as earrings.

French knitting is long and tubular, as opposed to conventional knitting, which creates flat pieces; it is achieved quickly and easily, and is produced using very few tools. It requires a spool and hook/needle. The main features of a French-knitting spool are the pegs that wire is wound around, and the central hollow channel the knitted piece is fed through. The diameter of the piece is determined by the diameter of this channel. A French-knitting spool usually has four or six pegs—the greater the number of pegs, the tighter and larger the knit produced; the larger the diameter of the hole, the larger the diameter of the knit. There are French-knitting spools designed specifically for jewelry wire work; however, many yarn versions can work just as well. Beads can be added in two ways (see page 85), to inject a colorful element.

PLAIN KNIT

For this technique, similar to traditional knitting, always work directly off the reel, and only cut when the piece of knitting is completed.

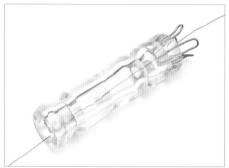

1. Insert a length of wire directly from the coil through the top of the French-knitting spool, into the channel, and out the other side. Pull the wire through so approximately 4 in. (10 cm) protrudes from the base.

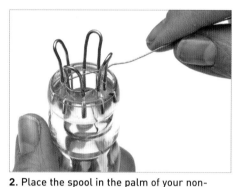

2. Place the spool in the palm of your non-dominant hand and hold the protruding wire. Take the longer (reel) end of the wire and wrap it around the first peg in a clockwise direction, leaving it quite loose. Repeat with the next three pegs, working in a counterclockwise direction around the spool.

3. Once all four pegs have been wrapped loosely, wrap the first peg again, above the first coil. Repeat this process until all four pegs have been wrapped—take care not to wrap it too tight. Now hold the wire end along the length of the spool, keeping it secure and out of the way.

4. Using a fine crochet hook, and starting with the looped wire peg to the right of the loops, grasp and gently pull the loop below, lifting it over the top loop, then release from the hook. Repeat for all four pegs, until all the pegs are left with single loops.

5. After each row of knitting, give the wire at the end of the spool a tug to stretch and even out the knit. Repeat the wire-wrapping process across the four pegs to produce the next row of knitting.

6. Continue the knitting process, repeating the steps until a length of French knitting begins to form in the hollow channel.

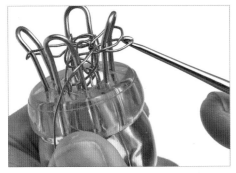

7. Once you have your desired length and a row of single loops on the pegs, use the crochet hook to bring the wire-end loop over to the peg to its right. This peg will now have two loops. Use the hook to pull the base over the top loop. Repeat by hooking this loop to the next peg, and again bring the base loop over the top loop. Repeat until only one loop remains on one peg.

8. Release the final loop from the peg, then pull the knit upward and out of the hollow channel. Tie a knot with the wire end before holding the piece by the two wire ends and giving it a slight pull in opposite directions. This will straighten the length of the knit piece.

This knit piece can be connected to other parts with the two wire ends.

FRENCH KNITTING WITH BEADS

The addition of beads can add color and value to a piece of jewelry. There are two ways to add beads to a French-knit piece.

The first method is to knit the beads into the body of the piece so they are visible on the outer surface. Uncoil a length of wire and thread on a desired quantity of beads. Proceed with the French-knitting technique described at left, but guide a bead (or beads) between each loop.

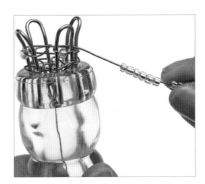

The finished beaded piece. The wire ends can be used to connect this to other components.

Another (very quick and easy) method of adding beads to French knitting is to insert them into the hollow center of the knit section. Knit a row then a bead into the center. Continue to knit and insert beads as you go. To ensure neat and evenly spaced beads, pull the end of the wire to straighten it and allow the bead to fall into the center naturally.

Macramé

Macramé is a traditional technique that involves the knotting of yarn or cord to create lengths and areas of patterned textiles. Products made from macramé range from clothing, blankets, and baskets to pieces of furniture—and the iconic friendship bracelet. With its decorative features and its ability to secure beads, macramé lends itself well to jewelry making.

The beauty of macramé is not restricted to yarn and cord—wire works very well, adding a more ornate and precious quality to the craft. Macramé essentially requires no tools, but you will need a kind of clamp to secure the wires in place during the knotting process. Wire is less flexible and malleable than yarn, and through tying and knotting it will become tempered. Therefore, macramé knots created with wire should start off much looser than their yarn equivalents, and a more gentle, gradual, and measured knotting process should be adopted to achieve neat and even patterns.

As with other wire-working techniques, the macramé design can be altered dramatically by adapting the wire type and color, or simply by working looser or tighter knots. Weaving beads or other nonmetal components within the knots can also have a profound effect on the finished product.

Before starting to work wire macramé, decide on the length of the finished piece and multiply this by seven or eight, which will result in an approximate length of wire needed. Of course, the necessary length will depend on the tightness of the knots and the thickness of the wires used, and additional wire ends are required to thread beads or to loop the ends. Always allow extra length for finishing the piece. There are many macramé knot types and techniques; shown here is one of the most common. You can use this technique to create the Macramé Necklace on pages 120–122.

Tips: Familiarize yourself with the knotting techniques using cord, which will give you confidence before you start working with wire.

Keep the knots the same by applying the same pull and pressure when knotting each one. Over- and underpulling will result in an uneven length and width of pattern.

The ends of the central wire of this complete piece can be shaped and formed to allow it to be connected or suspended.

SINGLE-KNOT MACRAMÉ

This version of macramé, although it looks complicated, is actually pretty straightforward. This type of knotting produces a three-dimensional body, so it is ideal for suspensions such as earrings or pendants.

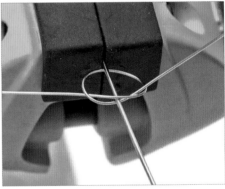

1. Cut a 4 in. (10 cm) length of 20-gauge (0.8 mm) round wire, and insert ¾ in. (20 mm) into a vise to secure it in place. Bring a 36 in. (90 cm) length of 22-gauge (0.6 mm) wire and place the center point perpendicularly under the thicker wire. Cross the right-hand wire end over the central secured wire then feed the left-hand wire over the right wire and under the central wire to tie a loose knot. Guide the loose knot upward along the length of the central wire.

2. Once the first knot has been completed, repeat and create a second knot, again taking the right-hand wire and crossing it over the top of the central wire. Pull the knot upward along the length of the central wire until it sits neatly under the previous knot.

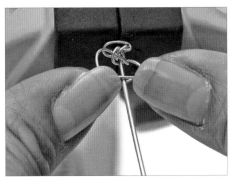

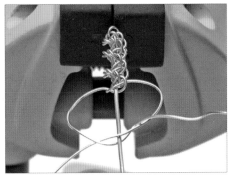

3. During the process of tying the first few knots, the piece will naturally want to pull forward. To avoid the knots detaching from the central wire, keep it in place and as close to the vise as possible with your thumb during the manipulation of the wire. As the length of knots increases, it will become stable and secured.

4. Continue knotting, always creating the loose knot quite far along the length of the central wire. This will allow you to tighten and feed the knot upward in a neat and uniform manner, creating a perfect knot that sits precisely below the first knot.

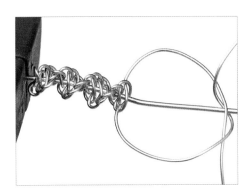

5. As the knots start to increase they will form spirals along the length of the central wire. To keep the size of the spirals uniform, tie each knot and tighten using the same tension and pull as the previous one. Any inconsistencies in the process of knotting and tightening the wire will be reflected in the final piece, with irregular and uneven lengths of spirals.

6. Once the desired length of spirals has been achieved and the two narrower wires are approximately 3 in. (70 mm) in length—any shorter and it would be difficult to grasp to tie an even knot—wrap one end around the central wire beneath the last knot two or three times. Take the second wire end and wrap it around two or three times after the previous coils. Secure by squeezing the ends with chain- or flat-nose pliers.

ALTERNATING KNOTS

An alternative macramé technique that can be used with wire is the Alternating Knots technique. The same system of knotting is applied as in the Single-Knot method, but the way the wires are crossed over varies.

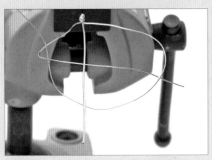

1. Secure your wires in a vise, as with the method at left. As you begin to knot, first the left wire goes over the top of the central wire and the right wire crosses over the top and under the central wire.

2. On the next knot, the right wire is passed over the central wire and the left is brought under the right and central wires.

3. Once you have reached the desired length, wrap and secure your wires as at left. You can also use nylon-coated flat-nose pliers to tidy, straighten, and temper the piece.

4. This knotting technique produces a flat length of knots, and is ideal for further shaping or to sit flush against the wearer; it is excellent for bangles and rings.

Wire twisting

The process of twisting wire creates neat and attractive decorative detailing, while adding strength. This twisting technique can be carried out on a single strand of shaped wire, or two or more strands can be combined together. A simple square-profile wire can be turned into a more ornate piece with "diamond cut" features. Simply by adjusting the number of twists or rotations along the piece, you can achieve very different finishes.

Twisted wire is created by securing one end of a length of wire and twisting from the other end. In theory, this is a basic technique that is quick and easy, but in practice, it can prove difficult to achieve an even and consistent finish, especially with heavier and shaped wire. To successfully make uniform twisted pieces, a tool such as a handheld drill is essential. Handheld drills, electric drills, wire-twisting pliers, and swivel-head pin vise drills are commonly used for wire twisting.

A handheld drill is ideal for creating twisted wire, offering much more control than an electric version. You can control the tension and stop twisting when necessary. Though an electric drill may speed up the process, there is less time to react and stop twisting when you want to; an electric drill is also more dangerous. In comparison to a swivel-head pin vise drill, the handheld drill is capable of gripping and securing heavier shaped wire and multiple strands.

Once you've finished twisting, the length of wire can be further shaped and formed into main parts of jewelry such as bangles or neckpieces, or applied as components of a larger piece. Because twisting strengthens a piece, it can be ideal for creating parts that can endure much pressure and strain—for example, in bangles and rings; however, the ornamental features and aesthetic detailing of twisting make it fitting for any jewelry piece. Note that the final length of a twisted piece is roughly half the length of the original wires, depending on the tightness of the twists.

Caution: When wire is twisted, it becomes tempered and hard. The wires can snap and cause injury. Wear protective eyewear when doing this technique.

SINGLE-STRAND TWIST

Square, rectangular, or D-section wires all make for an interesting single-wire twisted piece.

1. Insert a 3 in. (80 mm) length of 20-gauge (0.8 mm) square-section wire into the chuck of the handheld drill. Ensure the wire is pushed into the chuck as far as possible so it touches the back before securing it in place by tightening the chuck piece.

2. Remove any jaw protectors from the vise, as this will offer greater grip. Insert the opposite end of the wire into the jaws of the table vise by at least ½–1 in. (15–20 mm) to ensure it is held securely. Close the vise jaws as tightly as possible to secure the wire in place.

3. Pull the hand drill gently away from the vise so the wire is straight and taut. Wind the handle of the vise forward slowly and continue until you have the desired twist—either loose and relaxed or tight and detailed.

4. Release the vise jaws and the twisted wire, but make sure you are holding the wire end first. During the twisting process the wire will become tempered and rigid, making it likely to spring toward you when released—so extra care should be taken to avoid injury.

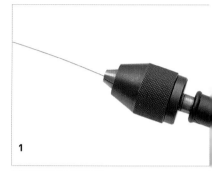

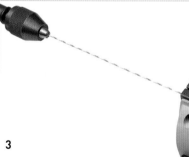

MULTI-STRAND TWIST

Multicolored strands of wire in different sizes will create elaborate and detailed twisted wire.

1. Often two different gauges of wire are difficult to secure in the chuck of the drill, but twisting the two together first will ensure that the narrower wire does not slip out during the twisting process. Use chain- or flat-nose pliers to secure the wires together.

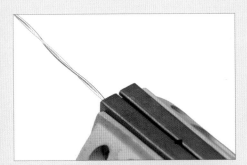

2. Insert the secured wires into the chuck of the handheld drill and secure by tightening. Again, pull the drill away from the vise and start to rotate the drill handle forward. The two wires will begin to wind together to create a multicolored twist. Continue until the desired twist is achieved.

3. Remove the piece from the vise, taking care to place your hands in front to keep the piece from flying forward. Use wire cutters to cut the two ends so only a neat twist remains at both ends. Variations can be created by using different wires.

LOOP-ENDED TWIST

A length of twisted wire with a loop end is very useful for attaching to other parts. This method also holds the wire more securely for twisting.

1. Cut a length of wire. Here, 28 in. (70 cm) of 20-gauge (0.8 mm) round wire has been used, but you can try different lengths and gauges. Fold the wire in half and insert both ends into the chuck of the drill. Tighten to secure the two ends in place.

2. Insert a metal rod (here a knitting needle was used) with the right diameter vertically into a table vise, and tighten to secure it in place. Thread the loop end of the wire into the rod. Pull the drill away from the vise to straighten the wire before beginning to rotate the drill handle forward.

3. Continue to wind slowly, as the twisted wires will become tempered. Slow rotations will allow you to sense the tension and avoid rapid overtwisting, which may cause the wires to become brittle and snap. Once the wires are wrapped tightly and a perfect round loop has been formed at the rod, remove the rod from the vise and drill before sliding the twisted piece off the needle.

4. Once the piece has been removed you will have a perfectly twisted length of wire with a complete round loop, which is ideal for attaching to other pieces of jewelry. If a loop is not required, remove it with wire cutters to reveal a perfect length of twisted wire.

Completed wire twists

Handmade chain

A chain is a length of connected links or loops that are secured together but can move freely. Chains are often used to connect jewelry components together, but they can also be a finished piece of jewelry, used on their own or as multiple strands.

Commercially manufactured chains are available in almost every size, link shape, length, type of metal, color, wire shape, and gauge imaginable. Chains are sold in coils and cut to the desired lengths, or are constructed as a completed piece with clasp fittings pre-attached, and can be bought from any good jewelry supplier. Often a commercially produced chain will work with a piece; however, sometimes a design can be greatly enhanced with the addition of a handmade chain.

A handmade chain will allow the maker total control over the style, length, and fit. At the design stage, consider how to link the units to ensure security and flexibility. The joints must be secure and not catch on clothing or on the wearer, as anything protruding may pull the chain links apart.

The links of a handmade chain can be freeformed using pliers, or created using a jig. With no soldered joins, handmade wire chains should be made from tempered wire; soft wire links would pull apart too easily. Each link should be identical, so you will need to be precise with your measuring and cutting. Showcased here are several types of chains made from round, square, and long hand-shaped wire links.

CHAINMAILLE

This technique is simply the linking of round jump rings to create strong lengths of chain. Chainmaille was originally employed as body armor due to its strong and resilient qualities, but it is now associated with jewelry chain making.

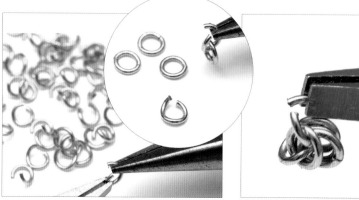

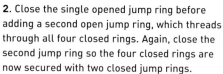

1. Take some unsoldered ⅛ in. (3 mm) 22-gauge (0.7 mm) jump rings, and use chain- and flat-nose pliers to open each one (see page 36). Close four jump rings so the ends meet perfectly. Hold one open ring with chain-nose pliers and thread all four closed rings onto it.

2. Close the single opened jump ring before adding a second open jump ring, which threads through all four closed rings. Again, close the second jump ring so the four closed rings are now secured with two closed jump rings.

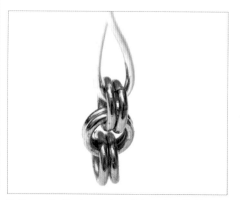

3. Separate the jump rings into pairs. Hold two of the original closed jump rings and let the other two hang. Thread a piece of wire through the two hanging jump rings; this will allow you to locate the chain end and hold it in place.

4. Hold the wired end in between your thumb and forefinger. Allow the other two closed jump rings to fall naturally downward before separating each, so one sits to either side. The middle two jump rings will now be visible.

The technique for handmaking chain is repetitive but systematic, and can be therapeutic. With very few tools you can create countless types of links and chains.

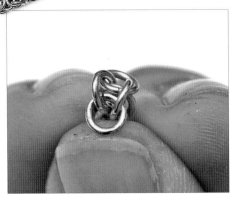

5. Using pliers or fingers, pull the two middle jump rings apart so the jump rings on either side will lift upward in the center. Use the tip of tapering fine-nose pliers to pull the middle two farther upward to allow access.

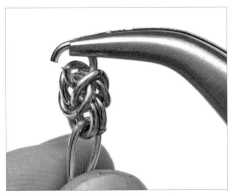

6. Using fine curved-nose pliers, grip an open jump ring and insert it into the two central jump rings. Once it has been threaded, close it shut using a second pair of pliers. Repeat with the second open jump ring so two closed jump rings become connected to the central rings.

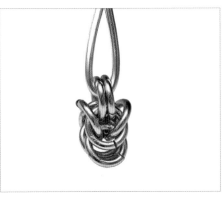

7. The eight connected jump ring piece will look like this. The two additionally connected jump rings sit flush with each other, held in place with the previous two jump rings. The beginning of the chain is starting to form.

8. To continue the process, the initial two-by-two-by-two jump-ring configuration must be presented by connecting four additional jump rings. To do so, connect two jump rings to the end of this piece, before repeating and connecting a further two jump rings.

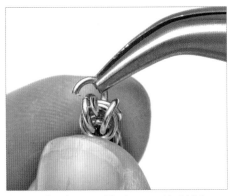

9. Turn the piece upside down and hold it in place. Repeat the previous steps and guide the two top jump rings to either side, and pull the middle two jump rings upward. Thread an open jump ring through the two central jump rings. Close and repeat with a second open jump ring.

10. Repeat the stages of linking a two-by-two-by-two jump-ring configuration, before connecting double jump rings to the central two jump rings. A length of chain will form; continue until your desired length is achieved. Finally, remove the scrap wire at the end.

LOOPED LINK CHAIN

This type of chain is very adaptable and can be worn around the neck or the wrist. Its simple shape allows additional parts, such as pendants or charms, to be easily connected. By simply using a heavier-gauge wire you can create a really strong and durable chain.

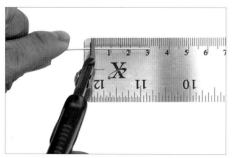

1. Cut 1¼ in. (30 mm) lengths of wire from tempered wire directly off a reel. Measure this first piece along a ruler and use this as a guide for the following lengths. Before cutting the second wire piece, use the flat side of the cutters to trim off the pinched end of the wire coil. Repeat this process after each 1¼ in. (30 mm) length has been cut to ensure both ends are flat, flush, and neat.

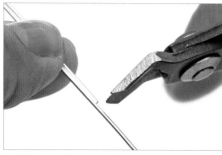

2. Using the first 1¼ in. (30 mm) wire piece as a guide, hold it against the straightened and tempered wire from the coil so the two are side by side. Cut with flat cutters, with the flat side facing away from the coil so the new cut piece will have flat ends. Repeat steps 1 to 3 until a large number of 1¼ in. (30 mm) lengths have been cut.

3. Use fine round-nose pliers to make a small loop at one end of the 1¼ in. (30 mm) wire, before moving to the other wire end. Make a loop that is the same size as on the opposite side, but perpendicular to the first loop. Repeat this process with all the 1¼ in. (30 mm) wire pieces.

4. With round-nose pliers, adjust the loops on both ends; grip and bend at a slight angle so the wire sits straight in the center of both. This changes the loops from a "P" to more of an "S" shape. Repeat this for all the pieces.

5. Insert the wire piece into the jaws of flat-nose pliers, to straighten and neaten it, making sure the two loops are perpendicular to each other. Repeat this process for all the pieces.

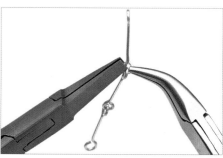

6. Continue to use flat-nose and curved chain-nose pliers to open the loop of each wire piece and connect it to the next. Close the loop and continue connecting and closing loops until the desired length of chain is achieved.

This length of chain is now ready to use for jewelry making.

TEARDROP HOOK CHAIN

The hook connection of this chain allows you to securely link each wire component. This results in a flexible chain that will mold to the wearer and sit around the wrist or neck comfortably.

1. As shown for the looped link chain (see left), cut a number of 1½ in. (40 mm) lengths of wire by measuring the first and then using this piece to help you cut the rest. Make sure the wire is straightened and tempered off the coil before cutting lengths.

2. Measure ½ in. (15 mm) from the end of the wire piece before gripping it with round-nose pliers. Hold the piece approximately one-third of the way along the jaws and, with your forefinger and thumb, pull the two wire ends downward, wrapping the wire around the plier jaws. Repeat for all the wire pieces.

3. Remove the shaped piece from the pliers and reposition by placing it flat between the jaws at the same jaw position as before. The pliers should hold the piece just below the wire end.

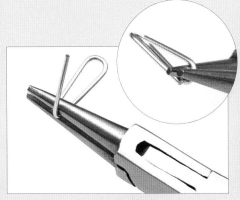

4. With the thumb and forefinger of your free hand, push the two ends upward around the top jaw of the pliers. Squeeze the two ends until the wire end and the curved part meet. Repeat for all the wire pieces.

5. To connect the components together, thread one of the links into another through the top wire end/opening. The design of this link allows each to be securely connected. Continue to connect further links until the desired length of chain has been achieved.

6. Once the desired length has been created, use your forefinger and thumb to squeeze the wire ends of each link/component. This will give greater security and keep the links from detaching.

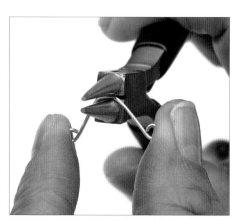

This completed chain can be connected to a clasp fitting or attached to another component.

PETALS CHAIN

Tha nature of the links in this chain gives it an irregular and interesting aesthetic. By connecting small beads across this chain in a scattered pattern, you can create a very detailed neckpiece.

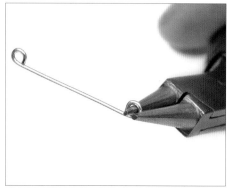

1. Cut a quantity of 1½ in. (40 mm) lengths of wire from straightened and tempered wire off the coil. Use round-nose pliers to grip and loop both ends. Both loops should be at similar angles.

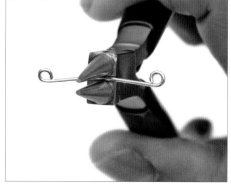

2. Place the center of the wire-looped piece into the jaws of the round-nose pliers with the front of the loops facing forward. Squeeze the pliers' handles to hold the piece in place.

3. While gripping the pliers and wire piece with one hand, use the fingers from the other to pull the two loop ends downward and around the lower jaw of the pliers. Push both ends so they cross over.

4. Put the piece into the jaws of flat-nose pliers (plain or nylon-coated) and squeeze tightly to flatten and straighten the shaped piece. Repeat steps 1 to 4 with all the cut wire pieces, and set them aside.

5. To connect each link, use curved chain-nose pliers to open the top right-side loop. Insert the left loop of a second shaped wire piece and close the first loop to secure both together. Continue repeating this connection process until the desired length has been created.

SQUARE COIL CHAIN

This chain offers not only an interesting type of link, but also added security in the connection of each link. The end shaped coil can be adapted to round or triangular shapes.

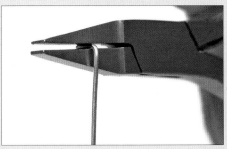

1. No pre-cutting of wires is necessary for these links; instead, work directly off a coil of wire. Temper and straighten a length of wire from the coil and then use flat-nose pliers to hold the end in place. Create a square shape by wrapping the wire around the pliers' jaws.

2. Continue to move and wrap the wire (still held by the pliers) around and below the first square-shaped coil. Feed and shape the wire around three times to complete a square coiled shape.

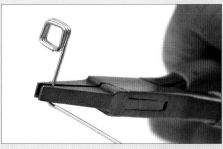

3. Measure ½ in. (15 mm) from the top of the square coil before creating another square shape. For a matching square, ensure the wire is held in the same jaw location as before.

4. Repeat the coiling process, wrapping the wire around three times. Once the base square coil is created, cut the wire end with cutters, with the flush side facing the piece. Repeat steps 1 to 4 until a quantity of these links have been created.

5. To connect each link, thread the top square coil onto the base coil of a second link. (Use the same process as for connecting split rings; see page 37.)

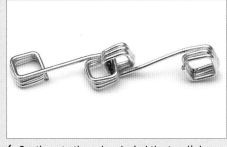

6. Continue to thread and wind the two links until they are joined completely. Once the two pieces have been linked together, the square coils may be a little loose or misshapen. If so, use flat-nose pliers to reshape them.

7. Repeat the linking process until the desired length of chain is achieved.

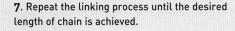
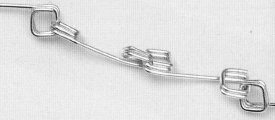

Tip: After cutting a shaped piece away from the coil of wire, and before starting to create the next link, use the wire cutters to remove the sharp end from the wire coil. This will ensure both ends of the shaped piece are flat and neat, preventing injury to the wearer.

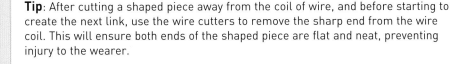

Finishing techniques

Once the main body of a jewelry piece has been completed, it often requires finishing techniques to attach it to findings that will allow it to be worn securely and comfortably. Parts may also need to be joined or fastened together, and wires play an important part in this.

As well as joining components together, findings are also used to cover unsightly finished ends, such as knit or wrapped wire areas, for a more professional finish. Finishing techniques are therefore essential skills to learn to make your pieces stand out.

Finishing may involve a simple joining technique, such as attaching the main feature to a clasp with the use of spilt rings, or it may be more complicated, involving a variety of findings and components. Additionally, a finishing technique may require the connection of a metal part to a nonmetal material such as cord or leather, or a combination of chain and wire. Whatever the finishing techniques used, choosing the correct findings and connectors is important in order to secure the parts together and result in a safe and wearable piece of jewelry. The types of findings used to finish a piece of jewelry are normally determined by the overall design, the desired function, and how much stress the piece will endure.

In this section you will learn to connect metal to metal, nonmetal materials to metal, and beads to metal to finish a jewelry piece beautifully and professionally.

Stringing/beading wire

Beads are perhaps the most likely nonmetal elements applied to add color to a piece of jewelry. Whether they are precious or plastic, with countless shapes, colors, sizes, and other features, beads are ideal and practical components to add value to a piece.

To thread strands of beads, beading wire or thread is used. Metal beading wire is available in a variety of types and colors—it is both strong and malleable, making it well suited to longer lengths.

Beading wire, unlike regular jewelry wire, is made up of a number of wires twisted together. These fine twisted wires, along with the nylon coating, make this type of wire extremely strong but flexible. The higher the number of internal fine wires, the greater the flexibility and strength of the beading wire; however, this will also increase the cost of the wire. Therefore, do consider the purpose of the beading wire before making your selection; expensive beads should be held together with wire, components, and findings of an equal quality. Additionally, a piece that is worn often may benefit from higher-quality wire.

ATTACHING FINISHING COMPONENTS TO A BEADED CHAIN

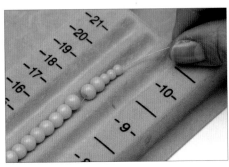

1. Use a bead board to plan the arrangement of the beads. Position the beads along the channels and move them around until you have an arrangement you are happy with. Consider positioning smaller-sized beads at both ends. This will allow the beads to pass through certain finishing components at a later stage.

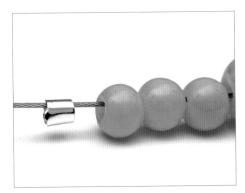

3. Select the correct-sized crimp that will allow space to thread the beading wire through twice. To keep a clasp in place, thread a crimp over the end of the beading wire and then feed the clasp through, before bringing the wire back into the tube of the crimp. Pull the wire end tight so the clasp is sitting as close to the last bead as possible.

Crimps

Crimps are small, ring- or tube-shaped pieces of metal that wire is threaded through; the crimp is squeezed down to secure it in place and acts as a "stopper," keeping beads from moving, or keeping two pieces of wire together, or enclosing and securing a finding such as a clasp. They are available in various sizes, metals, and colors.

ATTACHING CRIMPS

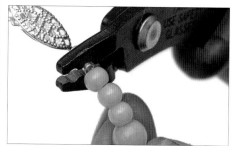

1. Once the crimp and clasp or other components are in place, position the crimp into the back of the crimping pliers and squeeze the handles of the pliers so the jaws press down hard onto the crimp. The crimp is now secured.

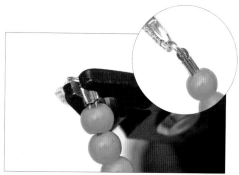

3. Place the flattened crimp into the front grooved part of the crimping pliers' jaws in a vertical position, and close to bend it in half, making the crimp smaller. The crimp remains fixed, and the clasp and beads are secured in place.

2. The crimp will become flattened in the center from the crimping pliers, and will be fixed in place, keeping the two wires from moving. The connected clasp or other components are also now secured and in place. The parts of the crimp that retain their shape are the areas where the two wires run through.

4. The protruding wire can be removed with wire cutters. Use strong, resilient cutters suitable for beading wire, which is made from steel and can easily damage fine wire cutters. Take care not to cut into the main wire, which is holding the beads in place. Before you complete the other side, shape the length around an object with a diameter similar to the wrist or neck—if the piece is crimped in a straight position it will become too tight when the piece is worn.

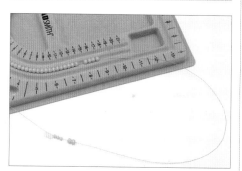

2. Cut a length of beading wire long enough to hold all the beads, with an additional 6 in. (15 cm) at either end. Attach a piece of masking tape 6 in. (15 cm) from one end of the wire; this will keep the threaded beads from escaping. Start to thread the beads onto the wire at the other end.

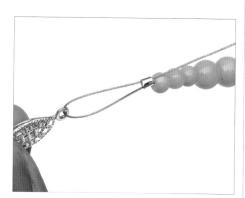

4. Bring the wire from the crimp and feed it through approximately 2 in. (50 mm) of beads. Bring the wire end out of the last bead of the 2 in. (50 mm) length.

USING CRIMPS TO SECURE COMPONENTS IN PLACE

Crimps can be used to keep beads from moving around, effectively acting as spacers.

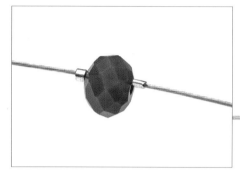

1. Locate the area where you want the beads, and thread on a small crimp. The crimp should be as small and discreet as possible, but not so small that it falls through the holes in the beads. Squeeze with chain-nose pliers to flatten and secure in place.

2. Thread the bead, pushing it along as far as it will travel, next to the flattened crimp. Thread another crimp and again flatten with flat-nose pliers to secure the crimp and lock the bead in place.

3. Continue with as many beads along the length as you like. The length of beaded wire can be connected to a clasp to complete a necklace or bracelet, or be used as a jewelry component—for example, in earring drops.

CRIMP COVERS

Crimp covers are applied to obscure crimps to make the finished piece of jewelry look more professional. These covers are available in many colors and sizes. Before applying a crimp cover, ensure there is a small space between the clasp and the component.

1. Apply the crimp cover. If the opening is slightly too small, open it up by inserting the tip of fine-nose pliers and pulling the jaws apart. This will create a larger opening to allow it to be inserted over the crimp.

2. Hold the crimp cover in place, with the opening facing up. Use chain-nose or crimping pliers to close the crimp cover. To ensure the two ends meet perfectly, squeeze the cover from the side and then move the jaws around to the opening before squeezing it fully closed.

3. Squeeze the jaws gently at the opening to ensure the cover is sitting straight and that the two ends meet flush and not at an angle. The cover is now a perfect sphere that covers the crimp and makes for a much neater finish.

Wire protectors

Over time, the stresses that jewelry is exposed to will wear away the nylon coating on beading wires, and eventually the wire will break.

WIRE GUARDS

Wire guards protect the wire where it is likely to experience high levels of friction from an adjacent component.

1. Thread the crimp onto the wire and insert the wire guard. The wire should enter through one end at the top of the "U"-shaped wire guard and thread completely to the other end, passing outward.

2. Once the beading wire is threaded through the other end of the guard, hook it onto the connecting component. Shown here is a round clasp end, which the wire guard is joined to, before the beading wire is fed through the crimp from below.

3. Pull both ends of the wire, while securing the crimp in place, to tighten to the desired position. Squeeze the crimp with chain-nose or crimping pliers, following the previous crimping instructions. The clasp end is connected by the protected beading wire and the secured crimp. Any friction between the beading wire and the clasp end is now reduced by the wire guard.

FRENCH WIRE

French wire (like the wire guard) is used to cover and protect a section of beading wire where it is connected to a component, at the point of greatest stress. Made from tiny spirals of wound fine wire, this tubular product is sold in lengths in varies sizes, metal types, and colors. French wire is lightweight but extremely durable.

The coils of French wire are extremely delicate, and once shaped cannot be reshaped. Because of this, care must be taken during application or when it is stored. Its hollow body can be easily

damaged or squashed, so when not in use store it loosely in a hard container. Applied in the same way as a wire guard, a length of French wire is cut, threaded through the beading wire, and then positioned where the join will occur.

Cut a ⅜ in. (10 mm) length, and thread the crimp and then the French wire, before connecting to the attaching part. Follow the same steps as for the wire guard to connect and secure the parts together.

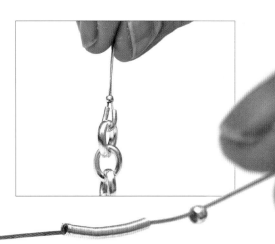

Calottes

Calottes are often applied to beaded pieces of jewelry to hide knots or crimps. They can be useful for gathering and securing a number of wires together. With an opening cap that shuts to enclose the knot or crimp, this component is ideal for disguising unsightly areas, and the looped end can be connected easily to another component. Calottes are available with and without an open hook loop, or with an attached round link.

CALOTTES AND CRIMPS

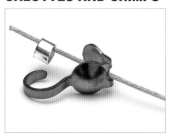 

1. Thread a calotte onto the wire and crimp at the desired position. Pull the calotte over the crimp to cover it, then close and squeeze tight with chain-nose pliers. This is now ready to be connected to another part.

2. To attach a part to the calotte, the loop is opened with pliers. The part is joined and the loop closed to secure the two together.

CALOTTES AND BEADING THREAD

A calotte can be used to cover a knot on beading thread. This makes it ideal for knotted beading, such as pearl bead work.

As with the wire, thread the calotte onto the thread and tie a knot. Make the knot stronger by tying another. Cut any excess thread and then bring the calotte to where the knot is. Close the calotte over the knot by squeezing it with pliers.

This shows how the calotte can be utilized in a beaded piece.

Rings

Rings are essential in jewelry making, and especially in wirework.

JUMP RINGS

Used to connect components together, and easy to produce in a variety of wire types and colors, jump rings can be freely adapted for any piece of jewelry. The lack of soldering in wirework jewelry means that more innovative methods of connecting parts and components together are necessary to ensure finished pieces are fit for wear. Jump rings' uses are limitless—connecting clasps and findings, joining multiple chains, connecting looped parts, beads, and charms—and the list goes on.

Here, separate components have been joined with jump rings to create an earring.

To use jump rings, always open them using two pairs of pliers, as shown on page 36. Feed all the necessary parts in the desired order onto the jump ring before closing it, again using pliers. Note: Do consider the weight of the components attached to the jump ring. If the parts are heavy and quite substantial in size, they may be better supported with a split ring.

SPLIT RINGS

Split rings are effectively double coiled rings with an opening on either side. They can be used to connect parts together by gently prizing one opening apart and threading it through the components. Split rings are stronger than jump rings, as they are unable to open and become disconnected; however, they are also heavier than jump rings so are not always appropriate. Jump rings are ideal for connecting lightweight and few parts, while split rings can be beneficial for heavier parts that may be exposed to more extreme wear and stress.

Split rings are opened with split-ring tweezers or pliers. Some split rings can also be easily opened with fingernails. Once a gap is achieved between the two rings, the connecting part can be threaded through. Hold this part in place to maintain the gap before adding additional components. Push and guide the parts all the way around the split ring until they are linked through the center.

Split rings are exceptionally useful for connecting an array of components; here are a number of chains joined together and held in place by one split ring.

ATTACHING CONES

Cones

Jewelry cones are used to cover the ends of multiple strands of wire, beads, or knit wire ends. These findings gather separate parts together and hide them discreetly, resulting in a more uniform and professional finish.

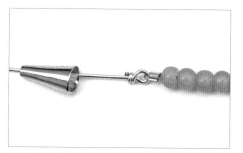

1. Thread the cone through the central wire of the piece until it covers the ends. Secure in place by creating a loop and winding the wire ends around it to finish. Cut any excess wire with wire cutters.

2. Always check that the beads you are using will fit into the cone. If the beaded piece uses beads that are too large, consider using small beads at the ends so the cone can fit over them.

Ribbon/Cord/Satin/Leather end caps

End caps, as shown on page 42, can be handmade with wire, or purchased commercially in "cup" or tubular versions. Whether they are attaching to leather, satin, or cord, cap ends are inserted and secured in place by squeezing the end together or applying a strong jewelry adhesive. Some end caps are designed with a central pin or screw that is inserted to hold the nonmetal part in place.

Folded-over crimp ends have a central part with two tabs on either end. Ribbon, cord, or leather can be inserted and then the two tabs folded over to secure the nonmetal material in place. The loop on the end is then used to join to another jewelry part.

To attach ribbon to a jewelry piece, flat tab caps are folded and secured to the end of a length of ribbon (see right). This keeps the ribbon from fraying and, with a loop ending, the ribbon can be joined to a clasp or a section of the jewelry piece.

FLAT TAB CAPS

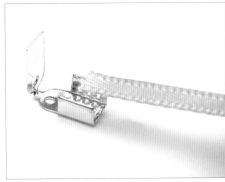

1. Select the correct size of ribbon crimp, matching the width of the ribbon with the internal width of the crimp. Insert until the ribbon end is fractionally below the top of the foldover. Use flat-nose pliers to fold one tab downward, and squeeze flat before folding the other.

2. Bring the top half-tab down and use flat- or chain-nose pliers to flatten down onto the previously secured tabs. The ribbon is now secured, and this attached piece can be connected to jewelry components via the hole at the top by the use of a jump ring, split ring, or threaded wire.

TUBE TAB CAPS

Cord ends are available with and without loops attached. These can also be with an open tab end, or the closed-ended tube type.

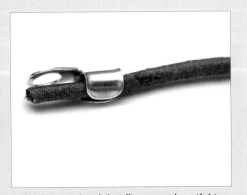

1. Select a cord end that fits securely; a tighter fit is better. Thread the cord through the opening channel and right through the other end. With flat- or chain-nose pliers, squeeze the side tabs together, securing the leather cord in place.

2. Cut any excess leather or cord with wire cutters, bringing it in as close as possible to give it a neat finish. This secured leather cord piece can now be connected by the loop end to other components.

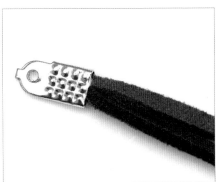

3. These types of ribbon ends can also be used for flatter lengths of suede or leather, or even multiple pieces of ribbon, as shown here.

3. Alternatively, this type of tubular cap end can be fitted to flatter pieces of cord, and then be secured by the previous method of using flat-nose pliers to flatten the tabs down.

CLOSED-ENDED END CAPS

With a single cord: Glue can be applied with a toothpick, a sewing needle, or a needle-ended tube (shown here). A two-part epoxy or other suitable jewelry glue will be the most effective. Apply a thin coat of glue into the inside of the cap and then push the cord or leather in. Make sure the cord or leather is pushed into the cap as far as possible. Allow to dry, following the instructions on the glue.

Tip: For lengthy tube ends, use a piece of wire or a toothpick to insert the glue; this will make it cleaner and easier to get it all the way in.

With multiple cords: Multiple strands of cord or leather can be secured and glued into one end cap as follows:

1. Gather the multiple strands and secure neatly with masking tape. Neaten the ends, and to prevent raveling, briefly hold a lighter to the ends (this only applies to strands of materials likely to ravel; leather or suede should not need this). This will melt the ends slightly to prevent further raveling and allow more secure bonding.

2. Apply a coating of glue to the cord ends, spreading it between the strands. Use an old pair of pliers to squeeze the strands together before applying more glue. The glue will run between the three strands and bind these together.

3. Apply a further light coat of glue to the inside of the cap end and push the multiple strands of cord into the cap. Push as far as possible and then let the glue dry. Once the glue has dried, remove the masking tape.

Chapter Three:
Projects

This chapter will explore creative applications of the techniques and skills presented in the previous chapter. The projects included have been created in a contemporary style, but use traditional techniques and a mixture of commonly used materials and beads. Each project combines several techniques and utilizes a numbers of tools and wire-making materials. With 11 projects and a selection of jewelry types, ranging from rings to brooches, you can choose to follow the project stages precisely in order to replicate the illustrated designs or, alternatively, take inspiration from each and adapt, develop, and create your own personal designs.

Twisted wire ring with crystal beads

By simply wrapping wire over a round form, you can create a ring shank very quickly and easily. Additional beads can then be secured to the main shank area to complete the beaded ring. A quick and easy project, with straightforward techniques and few tools required, this ring is an ideal first wirework project.

First, measure the finger the ring will be worn on using a ring sizer. Once you have the size, consider the actual area of the ring that will be visible on the top of the shank. Bear in mind that, when the ring is worn, only around a third of it will be visible from the top of the hand, and therefore only this area is suitable for beads. Any greater area of bead coverage will make the ring uncomfortable and impossible to wear.

When using nonprecious metals for close skin-contact jewelry, a nontarnishing metal such as silver- or gold-plated wire is ideal, as it will not discolor when worn against the skin—unlike some other metals such as copper. Whether you use a contrasting color combination of beads or a blend of similar colors, this ring works best with a mixture of types of beads.

You will need:

» 2 × 20 in. (50 cm) lengths of 20-gauge (0.8 mm) round, silver-plated copper wire
» 1 × 14 mm round faceted bead
» 4 × 6 mm round beads
» 1 × 6 mm round faceted bead
» 1 × 6 mm crystal bicone bead
» 1 × 3 mm crystal bicone bead
» 1 × oval crystal bead
» Ruler or tape measure
» Wire cutters
» Ring mandrel with ring-size indicators
» Chain-nose pliers

1. Take two 20 in. (50 cm) lengths of wire and thread the largest bead through to the center point. Pull both double wires tightly opposite each other underneath the bead to secure in place.

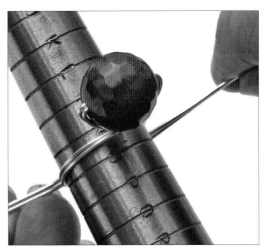

2. Position the bead on the ring mandrel at approximately six sizes above the desired size, and wrap the wires around once. Being careful not to cross the sets of double wires, bring both sets of wires back to the top of the ring mandrel.

3. Lead the left-side double wires underneath the bead and wrap them around tightly. Leave the ends to sit upward, along the length of the mandrel. Take the right-side double wires and wrap them around the middle bead and allow it to sit along the ring mandrel.

4. Thread five varying beads onto one of the double wires from the right side. Push the beads along the wire until they are sitting tight against the center before pulling the wire tightly upward to keep the beads from becoming loose.

Continues on next page

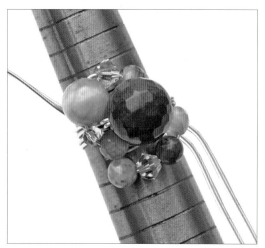

5. Take the other double wires and thread the remaining beads onto the outer wire. Pull the double wires downward to secure the beads. The two double wires should be sitting vertically opposite each other, one at the top and one below the central bead.

6. Taking the bottom double wire, wrap it around the central bead once and bring it to the right-hand side of the shank. Wrap it around the top of the shank twice. If the wire is difficult to manipulate, pull each of the two wires separately with either your fingers or the chain-nose pliers.

7. Repeat step 6 with the remaining double wires. Remove excess wire with wire cutters. To keep any sharp ends from making contact with the wearer, ensure that the wire ends on both sides are sitting flush with the outside of the shank and not on the inside.

8. Using chain-nose pliers, squeeze the wire ends toward the shank. Place the ring back onto the ring mandrel and reshape it if necessary. Flip over, and take care to do the same on the other side so the shank is uniform on both sides. Tap gently with a nylon- or rubber-ended hammer to reshape, if necessary.

Beaded earrings

These earrings comprise three main components linked and suspended from one another. The creation of separate parts that are linked together allows natural movement to occur during wear. The static beads, secured by wiring coiling along the hook attachment, draw the eye to their colors, while light catches the suspended beads below as the earrings move with the wearer.

Any pieces of jewelry that come in pairs, such as earrings or cufflinks, should always be matching, and mirrored if required. This particular earring design is made to be a symmetrical and identical pair, so to achieve uniformity, a mandrel is used. A ring mandrel is a practical piece of equipment that not only assists in the production of rings, but can also be used to shape varying sizes of curves and hoops. In this project, the mandrel allows the creation of identical matching central loops.

During the design process, think about the colors of the materials for the piece. In this particular project, gold-colored wire enhances the green and opalescent colors of the beads. The combination of the gold and green bestows a sense of luxury and opulence on the pieces.

You will need:

» 2 × 3½ in. (90 mm) lengths of 20-gauge (0.8 mm) round wire (earring hooks)
» 2 × 4 in. (10 cm) lengths of 22-gauge (0.6 mm) round wire (to wind and secure beads to hook)
» 6 × 4.5 mm round faceted green beads
» 2 × 3½ in. (90 mm) lengths of 20-gauge (0.8 mm) round wire (central hoop feature)
» 2 × round faceted opal-finish green beads measuring 8 mm × 6 mm
» 2 × 1½ in. (40 mm) lengths of 20-gauge (0.8 mm) round wire (central bead)
» 2 × 21-gauge (0.7 mm), 1½ in. (40 mm) length gold-colored head pins
» Ruler or tape measure
» Wire cutters
» Round-nose pliers
» Ring mandrel
» Chain-nose pliers
» Curved chain-nose pliers

Continues on next page

Tip: During the production of earring hooks, ensure that the pair matches and the curves are bent at the same point by forming them simultaneously. Alternatively, shape one and form the second by copying the same production stages and using exactly the same tools.

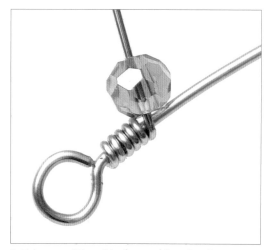

1. Take one of the 3½ in. (90 mm) lengths of 20-gauge (0.8 mm) wire, and loop one end before winding 22-gauge (0.6 mm) wire around from the end of the loop five times. Using the technique illustrated on page 62, secure two 4.5 mm beads onto the length of wire. Complete by winding and coiling the wire five times after the second bead.

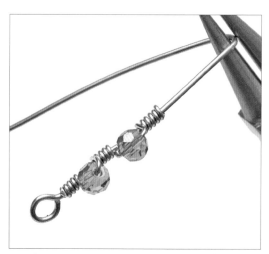

2. Using round-nose pliers, measure 1½ in. (40 mm) from the top of the loop, make a bend, and pull the wire downward. If extra security is required, take the pliers to the end of the wire and pull forward to create a curve at the end. This will keep the earring hook from easily falling out of the ear.

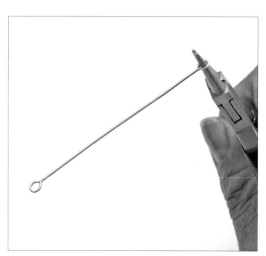

3. With another 3½ in. (90 mm) length of 20-gauge (0.8 mm) round wire, use round-nose pliers to create a loop that is approximately ⅛ in. (4 mm) in diameter on one end. Repeat the process on the other wire end so both ends are matching in size.

4. Place the length of wire around the ring mandrel at the size "Y" position. Bend and shape the wire around the mandrel with your fingers, and if necessary with a nylon-head hammer. Make sure the two loops sit flush against the mandrel. A ring is formed.

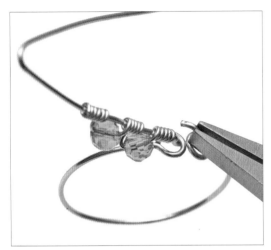

5. Open the loop at the end of the hook with chain-nose pliers and connect to the two loops of the ring. Once both loops have been joined, close the loop in the earring hook to secure in place.

6. Using 1½ in. (40 mm) of 20-gauge (0.8 mm) wire, create a loop at one end, about ⅛ in. (4 mm) in diameter. Thread through the largest bead and loop the wire at the other end, then cut off the excess wire. Open one loop and connect to the double loops of the ring.

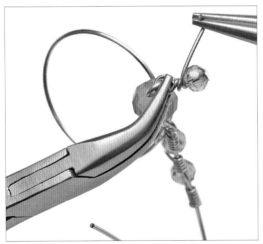

7. Thread the last small bead onto the head pin, create an open loop, and attach to the end loop of the central large bead. Wind the wire end of the head pin around the loop to close, and secure in place.

8. Repeat steps 1–7 to make a matching pair. Prior to wearing the earrings, don't forget to round off the edges of the wire hook to remove any sharp edges.

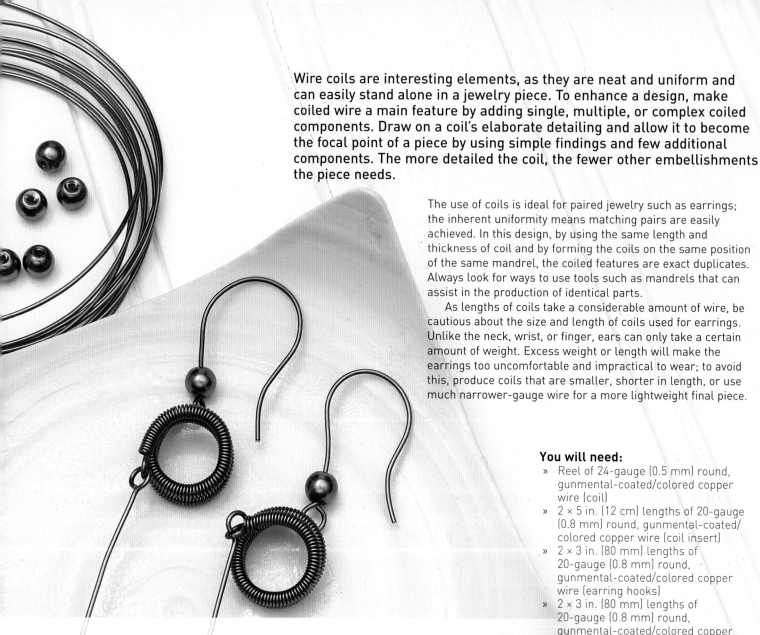

Wire coils are interesting elements, as they are neat and uniform and can easily stand alone in a jewelry piece. To enhance a design, make coiled wire a main feature by adding single, multiple, or complex coiled components. Draw on a coil's elaborate detailing and allow it to become the focal point of a piece by using simple findings and few additional components. The more detailed the coil, the fewer other embellishments the piece needs.

The use of coils is ideal for paired jewelry such as earrings; the inherent uniformity means matching pairs are easily achieved. In this design, by using the same length and thickness of coil and by forming the coils on the same position of the same mandrel, the coiled features are exact duplicates. Always look for ways to use tools such as mandrels that can assist in the production of identical parts.

As lengths of coils take a considerable amount of wire, be cautious about the size and length of coils used for earrings. Unlike the neck, wrist, or finger, ears can only take a certain amount of weight. Excess weight or length will make the earrings too uncomfortable and impractical to wear; to avoid this, produce coils that are smaller, shorter in length, or use much narrower-gauge wire for a more lightweight final piece.

You will need:

» Reel of 24-gauge (0.5 mm) round, gunmetal-coated/colored copper wire (coil)
» 2 × 5 in. (12 cm) lengths of 20-gauge (0.8 mm) round, gunmetal-coated/colored copper wire (coil insert)
» 2 × 3 in. (80 mm) lengths of 20-gauge (0.8 mm) round, gunmental-coated/colored copper wire (earring hooks)
» 2 × 3 in. (80 mm) lengths of 20-gauge (0.8 mm) round, gunmental-coated/colored copper wire (pearl wire drops)
» 8 × 8 mm round, fully drilled, mink-colored pearls
» Wire cutters
» Coiling tool
» Ring mandrel
» Round-nose pliers
» Chain-nose pliers
» Flat-nose pliers
» Wire cup burr

Wire coil earrings

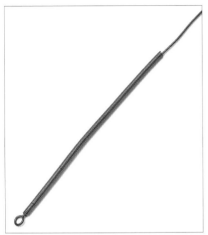

1. Use a reel of 24-gauge (0.5 mm) round wire and create a 4 in. (10 cm) coil length on the smaller cranking handle (see page 75). Cut a 5 in. (12 cm) length of 20-gauge (0.8 mm) round wire, loop one end, and thread through the coil. Loop the other wire end to secure the coil in place.

2. Taking one of the lengths of coil, wrap it around the top part of the ring mandrel so two coils are created and the ends cross over. The two loop ends will be sitting with just over a ¼ in. (8 mm) gap.

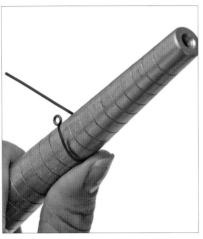

3. To create the earring hook, loop one end of a 3 in. (80 mm) length of 20-gauge (0.8 mm) wire before wrapping around size "J" of the ring mandrel. Remove and, using round-nose pliers, bend the unlooped end so it curves outward.

4. With the assistance of chain-nose or flat pliers, open the earring hook loop and connect to the top loop of the coiled bead component. Close the loop to secure the two parts together.

5. Use round-nose pliers to create a ⅛ in. (4 mm) loop on one end of a 3 in. (75 mm) length of 20-gauge (0.8 mm) round wire. Thread three pearls and loop the other end.

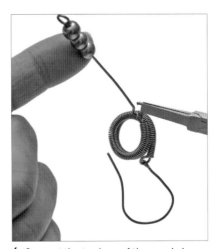

6. Connect the top loop of the pearl-drop part to the bottom loop on the coiled bead. Close the loop to secure and thread a single pearl onto the hook. Repeat steps 1–6 for the second earring.

Tip: Ensure the earring hooks are comfortable and safe to wear by filing the wire down with a cup burr tool.

This project is straightforward, with simple techniques that result in a professionally finished bangle design. The main bangle frame can be produced very quickly, so multiples in coordinating colors can be made quickly and worn together. If you like, you can suspend additional charms or beads from the main body of the bangle.

Wristwear endures great movement and strain during wear. It therefore requires the strength that twisted wire can offer, making this ideal for the main body of a bangle. It may appear that smaller gauges of wire will lack the strength necessary to withstand the pressures applied to a jewelry piece such as a bangle, but the simple technique of twisting more than one length of wire can provide the required durability. Also, the uniform slanted detailing achieved by the twisting makes an interesting feature and adds texture to the body of the piece.

Bear in mind when creating a bangle that, to ensure comfort, it should be sized for the individual wearer. Excess wire may result in the bangle feeling loose or falling off; too small and the piece will become tight and uncomfortable. Also, consider the size of beads in conjunction with the gauge of wire when making this bangle. Larger beads would look cumbersome and would make the bangle heavy and uncomfortable to wear.

You will need:

- » 24 in. (60 cm) length of 18-gauge (1 mm) round, gold-colored wire (main body of the bangle)
- » 1 × 6 in. (15 cm) length of 18-gauge (1 mm) round, gold-colored wire (beads connector)
- » 3 × 10 mm round faceted crystals
- » Ruler or tape measure
- » Wire cutters
- » Handheld drill
- » Round rod or drill piece (6–7 mm diameter)
- » Table vise
- » Fine round-nose pliers
- » Chain-nose or flat pliers
- » Bangle mandrel or a round form strong enough to wrap and shape wire around
- » Nylon-head hammer

Twisted bangle

1. Take a 24 in. (60 cm) length of 18-gauge (1 mm) gold-colored wire, bend it in half, and insert the two wire ends into the handheld drill. Following the techniques on pages 88–89, rotate the drill to achieve a tightly wound length of wire. Remove from the vise and cut both ends with wire cutters.

2. Use fine round-nose pliers to create the smallest possible loop on one end of the twisted wire. Then reposition the pliers to create the main curve of the hook.

3. With chain-nose or flat pliers, squeeze the loop on the end of the hook to decrease the size and make it as neat as possible. Doing this will allow the hook clasp to thread through the corresponding ring clasp.

4. Apply round-nose pliers to create a ¼ in. (6.5 mm) loop on the opposite wire end. Place the wire onto the bangle mandrel and shape it with your fingers and a nylon-head hammer.

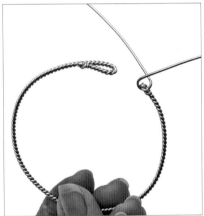

5. Take 6 in. (15 cm) of 18-gauge (1 mm) round wire and create a ¼ in. (5 mm) diameter loop 1½ in. (40 mm) from one end. Feed and connect to the loop on the bangle, and wind the wire end around the loop to secure this wire in place. Thread three beads onto the wire before creating a loop on the end, winding it closed to secure the beads and create the clasp end for the hook.

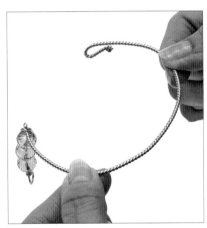

6. Once all the parts are linked, reshape the piece on the mandrel. Curve the beaded wire around the mandrel so the piece follows the natural curve of the wrist. Pull the two sides of the bangle outward to create pull and tension between the hook and ring upon connection.

Charm bracelet

A charm bracelet is characterized by the personalized miniature trinkets and adornments suspended from it, which showcase the wearer's individual style and personality. Historically, charms were used as amulets to ward off evil. Nowadays, charms are added over time, perhaps on a special birthday or to symbolize a hobby.

In this project, each wire charm is freeformed using hands and pliers (using skills learned in the Techniques section, pages 24–103). To produce accurate shapes, a sketch of the desired design is first created on paper (see pages 144–145 for design templates of all the charms featured in this project). This will also enable pieces to be exactly replicated in future.

Unless you are working with very fine wire, avoid shapes that have very sharp bends. The charms from this project are quite lightweight; for heavier-weight charms, use a heavier-gauge wire or square-profile wire for more weight and definition. (Bear in mind that you then won't be able to achieve such fine details.)

Each charm has been designed with a simple round bolt clasp that allows it to be disconnected from one part of the bracelet and reattached elsewhere, or connected to a different chain.

Have fun and use your imagination to create a selection of personalized charms that reflect your own interests and passions.

You will need:

» 7.5 in. (20 cm) chain—a loose chain that is not too lightweight, or a completed bracelet of choice
» Toggle-and-ring clasp fitting—for an uncompleted length of chain
» 1.1 yd (1 m) of 20-gauge (0.8 mm) round, silver-colored copper wire
» 1.1 yd (1 m) of 24-gauge (0.5 mm) round, silver-colored copper wire
» 5 × 20-gauge (0.8 mm) 1½ in. (4 cm) head pins
» 4 × 4 mm round, gray, faceted beads
» 1 × 14 mm flower-shaped faceted bead
» 6 × 7 mm round bolt rings
» Paper (graph or plain) and pen or pencil, for sketching
» Ruler or tape measure
» Wire cutters
» Flat-nose pliers
» Chain-nose pliers
» Ring-nose pliers
» Round-nose pliers (large and small)

LETTER CHARM

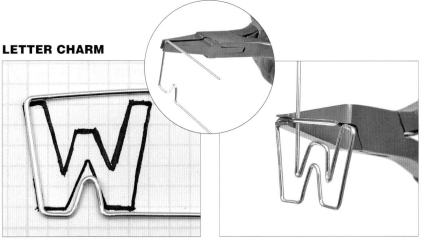

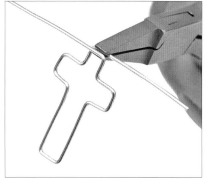

1. Sketch the letter wanted at the desired size. Alternatively, print a template out or use the templates on pages 144–145. Repeat this process for all other charms as necessary. Starting with a 5½ in. (14 cm) length of tempered 20-gauge (0.8 mm) wire, make a 70-degree bend with flat-nose pliers 1 in. (25 mm) from the end. Move the pliers along the wire, following the design and copying the bends.

2. Continue to shape the wire. Once your chosen letter is complete, the two wire ends should meet. Wrap one wire end around the other and create a loop with the remaining wire. Wrap the wire around the base of the loop to secure. Cut away any excess wire with wire cutters and squeeze in place with chain-nose pliers.

CROSS

1. Cut a 5 in. (13 cm) length from the tempered 20-gauge (0.8 mm) wire. With flat-nose pliers, hold the wire at the midpoint. Bend both ends at a right angle to create two parallel wire ends. Continue moving the pliers down along the length of one wire end before bending and shaping to create a cross. (Continued below.)

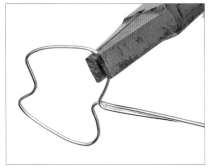

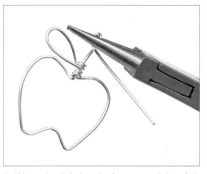

2. To make the shape match on both sides, bend one side first and then mirror the bends on the other side. Complete the piece at the top by wrapping the wire around the other wire end and then looping the other end, before wrapping below the loop to close and secure the wire. Cut off any excess wire with wire cutters and secure by squeezing tightly with flat-nose pliers.

APPLE

1. Cut a 5½ in. (14 cm) length of tempered wire. Start shaping from the middle of the 20-gauge (0.8 mm) wire, creating a curve at the base. Work with ring-nose and round-nose pliers to form one side of the apple, and repeat on the other side, making it not quite symmetrical. Bend the wire ends so they sit vertically, parallel to each other.

2. Wrap the left-hand wire around the right twice, shape into a leaf, bring the wire end back to the middle, and wind around the other wire once more. Cut off any excess wire with wire cutters and squeeze in place with chain-nose pliers. With the remaining wire end, create a loop and then wrap around the base of the loop twice. Cut off excess wire and squeeze the wire ends.

Continues on next page

HEART

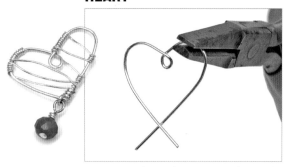

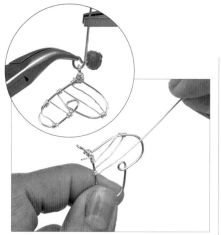

1. Cut 5½ in. (14 cm) of 20-gauge (0.8 mm) wire and, with round-nose pliers in the middle of the wire length, create a loop. Then, using ring-nose pliers with the curved face inside, form a heart. Bring both wire ends to the middle at a point. Take one wire end of the heart and wrap it around the other three times. Cut away the excess and secure the wire end with pliers. Create a loop on the other end and cut away the excess wire.

2. Use a 20 in. (50 cm) length of 24-gauge (0.5 mm) wire and secure it in place on the left side of the heart. Wrap sporadically across the heart and secure the end to the frame by wrapping three times. Cut away the excess and squeeze in place with pliers. Thread a ⅛ in. (4 mm) round faceted bead onto a head pin, loop the wire, and thread through to the loop on the heart before wrapping the head pin wire around itself to secure. Cut any excess wire.

FLOWER

1. Cut a 9½ in. (24 cm) length of tempered 20-gauge (0.8 mm) wire. Measure 1¼ in. (30 mm) from the end and create a round bend with round-nose pliers. Move the pliers along the wire approximately ½ in. (15 mm) and, using the top of the jaws, make another smaller bend. Continue to make bends and curves, always ensuring the top bend is larger so the wire shape begins to fan outward. (Continued below.)

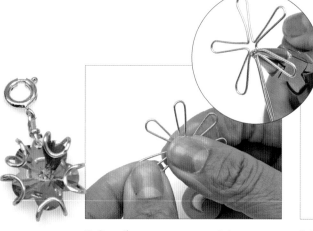

2. Once five curves are complete, use your fingers to pull and move each curve, spacing them outward until the piece resembles a five-petal flower. Use round-nose pliers and your fingers to neaten the piece by inserting the pliers into each "petal," and reshape as necessary. Use the pliers to bring the two wire ends to a join in the center, to meet and lie parallel.

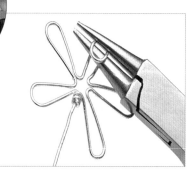

3. Take one wire end and wrap it around the other, then cut away any excess. Leave the other wire end. Move and space each petal shape to ensure the frame is as even and neat as possible. Grip the top of one petal with round-nose pliers and rotate the pliers inward to create a curve. Repeat this process for the other four petal shapes until you have a "claw"-type frame.

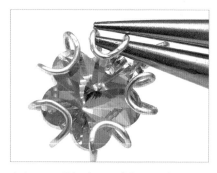

4. Insert a ½ in. (14 mm) flower-shaped faceted bead, bending in the petal shapes more if necessary with round-nose pliers to hold the stone in place. The five petal shapes will encapsulate the bead in the center. Then use the pliers to create a small loop above, and wind it around itself to secure. Remove any excess wire with wire cutters.

STAR

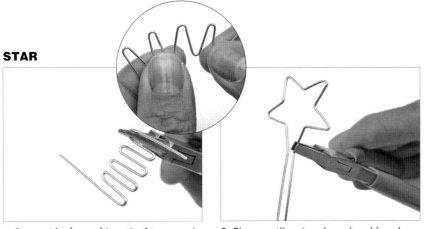

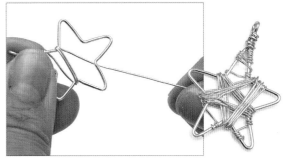

1. Cut a 5½ in. (14 cm) length of tempered 20-gauge (0.8 mm) wire. Use round-nose pliers to create a zigzag piece with four curves that are approximately ⅜ in. (10 mm) in length. Pull the curved shapes apart, open the piece outward, and manipulate with your fingers to create four points of a star.

2. Shape until a star shape is achieved. Use chain- or flat-nose pliers to bring the wire ends to a point to complete a five-pointed star. Angle the two wire ends so they meet together, wind one wire end around the other, and cut away any excess. Create a small loop with round-nose pliers on the other wire end, then wind the wire around itself to secure it.

3. Use the same wire-winding technique as for the heart shape, and crisscross approximately 15 in. (40 cm) of 24-gauge (0.5 mm) wire across this star-shaped frame. Once this sporadic winding is complete, secure the end by winding it around the frame three times. Cut away any excess with wire cutters, and secure it by squeezing with flat-nose pliers.

CONSTRUCTING YOUR BRACELET

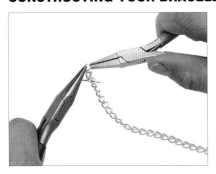

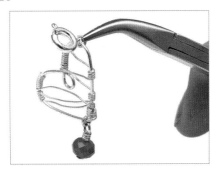

1. Once you have selected your length of chain, create the bracelet by attaching clasp fittings with jump rings, or split rings, or by wrapping securely with wire. Alternatively, you could use a store-bought bracelet.

2. Once all the charms have been completed, attach a bolt ring clasp to each charm by opening the ring gently, as you would with a jump ring, before connecting to the loops of each charm (or, as here, to one end of the heart frame). Close the bolt ring loop with pliers to secure it.

3. Each charm can be linked to a chain wherever you like. Here, between some of the charms, faceted beads have been suspended using head pins.

The main body of this necklace has been made using the macramé technique (see pages 86–87). The macramé knots provide a robust framework and hold the beads in place. Very few additional accents are necessary to complete this neckpiece: colored beads and a simple chain give this large pendant a contemporary look.

This necklace project involves very quick and simple techniques; once the macramé knots are complete, the remaining stages are quite straightforward. The knotting process is the most time-consuming stage of the production—however, once the technique is mastered, neat lengths of macramé knots are achievable fairly quickly and easily. The rule of thumb is to keep the tightness of the knots consistent to ensure a neat end result.

The use of gold-colored wire highlights the details of the twisted coil macramé knots, and coordinating colored beads keep the main focus on the central macramé knotted pendant. Additional shapes such as ovals or teardrops are easily formed from the knotted macramé lengths; however, do avoid angular shapes such as squares, rectangles, or triangles, as sharp corners are difficult to achieve and could damage the macramé knot detailing.

Macramé necklace

You will need:
- » 12 in. (30 cm) of 18-gauge (1 mm) round, gold-colored copper wire
- » 94 in. (240 cm) of 22-gauge (0.6 mm) round, gold-colored copper wire
- » 11 × 6 mm round faceted beads

- » 1 × 20-gauge (0.8 mm) diameter gold-colored head pin—1½ in. (40 mm) in length
- » 22 in. (56 cm) of ⅛ in. (3 mm) gold-colored curb chain
- » 2 × 5 mm jump rings
- » 1 × 8 mm gold-colored split ring
- » 1 lobster clasp, ⅜ × ¼ in. (9 × 6 mm)
- » Table vise or masking tape

- » Wire cutters
- » Tape measure or ruler
- » Bangle mandrel
- » Chain-nose or flat-nose pliers
- » Round-nose pliers
- » Curved-nose pliers

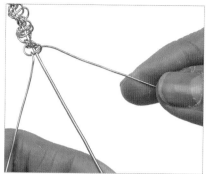

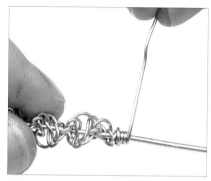

1. Secure a 7½ in. (19 cm) length of 18-gauge (1 mm) round gold-colored copper wire to the table with a table vise or masking tape. Create a 1½ in. (35 mm) length of single-knot macramé, leaving ½ in. (15 mm) from the end of the wire. A 24 in. (60 cm) length of 22-gauge (0.6 mm) round gold-colored wire is applied to create this 1½ in. (35 mm) length of knotted macramé.

2. Once the length of macramé has been created, wind one end of the wire around the central wire two or three times, and do the same with the other wire end, over and above the first coils. Cut both wire ends with wire cutters, then use chain nose pliers to squeeze the ends in place.

3. Thread two 6 mm round faceted beads onto the central wire and push them along until they sit directly below the wound wire ends. Make sure the beads sit as close to the wire coils as possible.

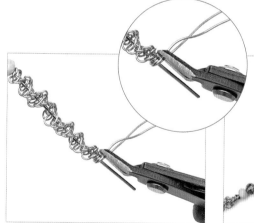

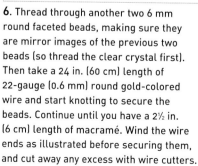

4. Cut a 36 in. (90 cm) length of 22-gauge (0.6 mm) round gold-colored wire and continue to tie single-action macramé knots directly below the two beads. This second section of macramé knots will secure the two beads in place. Continue to knot until a 2½ in. (6 cm) length of macramé knots is achieved.

5. Once a 2½ in. (6 cm) length of macramé knots has been achieved, repeat the process and wrap the two wire ends around the central wire before cutting away the excess. Use chain- or flat-nose pliers to squeeze and secure the wire ends.

6. Thread through another two 6 mm round faceted beads, making sure they are mirror images of the previous two beads (so thread the clear crystal first). Then take a 24 in. (60 cm) length of 22-gauge (0.6 mm) round gold-colored wire and start knotting to secure the beads. Continue until you have a 2½ in. (6 cm) length of macramé. Wind the wire ends as illustrated before securing them, and cut away any excess with wire cutters.

Continues on next page

7. Shape the length of macramé and the beaded part around a bangle mandrel. This piece, even with the macramé knots, should remain quite soft and malleable, so only use your fingers to form it. Avoid using a hammer, as this will distort and damage the macramé.

8. Once a round frame is formed, use round-nose pliers to create a small loop, with an outer diameter of approximately ⅛ in. (3 mm), on the left-hand wire end. Cut away any excess wire with wire cutters. With the other end, make a loop of about ¼ in. (6 mm) outer diameter; wrap the remaining wire below the loop twice. Cut away any excess wire. Reshape the frame on the bangle mandrel if necessary.

9. Open the smaller loop with curved-nose pliers to connect the opposite loop. Do so by connecting the larger loop from the base, below the wrapped wire, where the macramé ends and before the double-wrapped wire starts.

10. Cut a 2¾ in. (7 cm) length of 18-gauge (1 mm) round gold-colored wire and create an eye pin with a loop on one end with an outer diameter of about ⅛ in. (3 mm). Thread through six 6 mm round faceted beads before securing in place with a loop end. Thread through the loop onto the small loop at top of the round pendant piece, and wind the wire around to secure it. Remove any excess wire with wire cutters.

11. Connect a further 6 mm clear faceted bead to the end of the drop with a head pin. Thread and secure by winding the wire of the head pin around the looped end. Once connected, cut off any excess head-pin wire with wire cutters.

12. Thread a simple curb chain through the top pendant loop, and adjust the length accordingly; this piece has been made 22 in. (56 cm) long. Connect a clasp to one end and a split ring to the other with jump rings.

Beaded coil necklace

At first glance, it may be difficult to believe that only two gauges of wire and a few beads have been used to build this entire necklace, or that the strength required for the piece is achieved with only these materials and techniques. It is the wire wrapped around the main body of this piece that gives it its strength as well as making an interesting design feature.

Round-nose pliers are effective for creating curved and looped forms; however, to achieve uniform shapes that are consistently sized and distanced, a wire jig is more practical. A jig allows you to plan the location and size of each shape, as well as the distance between a curve, bend, or loop. This project illustrates how a main wire feature can be created using a jig, and attached as well as suspended from a simple handmade chain formed with only the use of pliers. Both techniques rely on wire shaping around a form—first a pegged jig for the body of the piece, and then the jaws of the pliers for the handmade chain.

Creating handmade chain is a wonderful technique that draws on repetitive shaping of wire. This can be done with pliers or a jig. Often so much emphasis is placed on hand-making the main element of a design, but little thought is given to the chain it will hang from. This is why being able to make simple or elaborate chains can really enhance a piece, and elevate it to become something original and special.

You will need:
- » 16 in. (40 cm) length of 19-gauge (0.9 mm) black wire (main body of the piece)
- » 39½ in. (100 cm) length of 24-gauge (0.5 mm) black-coated copper wire (for wrapping main body of piece and clasp parts)
- » 2 × 14 mm round black beads
- » 1 × 12 mm round gray bead
- » 6½ in. (16 cm) length of 19-gauge (0.9 mm) wire (for ring part of clasp)
- » 2¾ in. (70 mm) length of 19-gauge (0.9 mm) wire (for toggle bar of clasp)
- » 60 in. (150 cm) length of 19-gauge (0.9 mm) black-coated copper wire (to create 48 figure-eight links for chain)
- » Wire jig and pegs
- » Ruler or tape measure
- » Wire cutters
- » Nylon-coated flat pliers
- » Round-nose pliers
- » Chain-nose pliers

Continues on next page

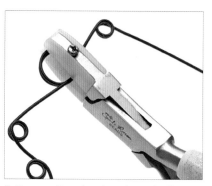

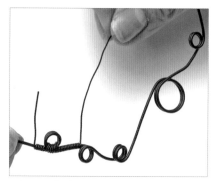

1. Insert four small pegs and one large one onto the jig in the configuration shown. Take a 16 in. (40 cm) length of 19-gauge (0.9 mm) round wire, and leave a good 3 in. (80 mm) before beginning to wrap around the first peg. Wrap around twice, then repeat the process across the remaining five pegs as shown.

2. Remove the wire piece from the jig and, using nylon-coated pliers and your fingers, reshape and straighten where necessary. Make sure to align the two coils of each double wrap so they sit on top of each other.

3. Start winding approximately a 30 in. (75 cm) length of 24-gauge (0.5 mm) round wire, ¼ in. (5 mm) along from the first left-sided loop. Take the wire around the base of the first loop and continue on the same level, along the piece, keeping the wrapping in the central wire.

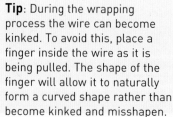

4. Once the wrapped coils reach the last loop, continue wrapping along a ¼ in. (5 mm) length. Cut away the excess and use chain-nose pliers to squeeze the wire end toward the central wire.

Tip: During the wrapping process the wire can become kinked. To avoid this, place a finger inside the wire as it is being pulled. The shape of the finger will allow it to naturally form a curved shape rather than become kinked and misshapen.

5. Thread a single black bead onto the left-side wire and loop the end before winding the wire to close. Remove any excess wire with cutters. Thread a single black and one gray bead onto the opposite side and repeat the process. The center feature of the necklace is now complete and ready to be applied to the chain at a later stage.

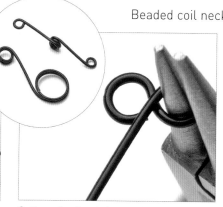

6. With the 6½ in. (16 cm) length of 19-gauge (0.9 mm) round wire, wrap around the first and second pegs on the jig twice to create the ring part of the clasp. To make the toggle, use the 3 in. (70 mm) piece of wire and, with round-nose pliers, follow the instructions on page 47 to create the bar component.

7. Take a 5 in. (12.5 cm) length of 24-gauge (0.5 mm) round wire and wrap it along the length of the bar of the toggle clasp. Repeat this wrapping process on the ring part of the clasp, making sure the wire ends of the loops are wrapped and secured. This will strengthen both parts. The two parts of the clasps are now complete and ready for connection.

8. To make the chain, uncoil a length of 19-gauge (0.9 mm) round wire and, using nylon-coated flat pliers, straighten and temper approximately 7 in. (18 cm). Create a flat end to the wire by cutting with the flat side of the cutters. Do not cut the wire, but rather work directly from the coil, making approximately 50 figure-eight links with round-nose pliers.

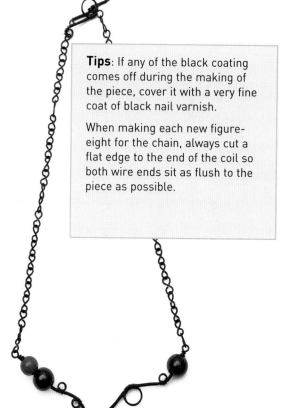

9. With the chain-nose or flat pliers, open one side of the figure-eight link and connect to another. Join together to create a length of 25 links, then repeat to produce a 23-link second length of chain.

10. Connect the shorter length of chain to the double-beaded loop side, and complete by joining the ring clasp and linking the smaller loop, leaving the larger side free. The longer length of chain is then joined to the single-bead loop side, and the toggle bar is attached from the lower loop to the chain.

Tips: If any of the black coating comes off during the making of the piece, cover it with a very fine coat of black nail varnish.

When making each new figure-eight for the chain, always cut a flat edge to the end of the coil so both wire ends sit as flush to the piece as possible.

Beaded barrette

Hair accessories, from everyday hairbands to elaborate one-off bridal hairpieces, can add something special to any outfit. This barrette is elaborate and detailed, with many beads and a crystal chain—perfect for a formal or special occasion. With a few minor changes—by making the piece smaller, adding fewer beads, or replacing the beads with a simple ribbon or bow—you could easily make a more casual piece.

It is generally best to use store-bought hair findings, as they are specially designed using strong metals and can grip the hair securely. Many also allow the connection of additional components. Do consider the weight of a hair accessory and the logistics of wearing it. Too heavy, and the piece will become uncomfortable to wear and may be impossible to secure. It is always good to work with a mirror, checking at various stages of production where parts will sit comfortably, securely, and looking their best.

This project perfectly illustrates how different gauges of wire can be utilized to form various areas of a piece, using different techniques. A main wire frame has been created from heavier 16-gauge (1.2 mm) wire—allowing the piece to retain its shape while offering a strong structure that the many beads can be joined onto—and fine, malleable wire is used to wind and secure beads and rhinestones in place.

You will need:

- » Silver-colored 2½ in. (60 mm) wide metal haircomb
- » 2½ in. (60 mm) length of ⅛ in. (3.5 mm) round rhinestone chain
- » 94½ in. (240 cm) of 24-gauge (0.5 mm) round, antitarnish, silver-plated copper wire
- » 20 in. (50 cm) of 16-gauge (1.2 mm) round, silver-plated copper wire
- » Approximately 32 flat round faceted ¼ × ⅜ in. (6 × 8 mm) beads
- » Approximately 74 flat round faceted ⅛ × ³⁄₁₆ in. (4 × 3 mm) beads
- » 4 in. (10 cm) of ⅛ in. (3 mm) round rhinestone chain
- » 4 × 3¼ in. (80 mm) head pins
- » ¾ in. (20 mm) of 2.5 mm chain
- » 1 × ⅜ in. (5 mm) round jump ring
- » Ruler or tape measure
- » Wire cutters
- » Round-nose pliers
- » Flat-, chain-, or curved-nose pliers
- » Bangle or round form—to shape wire if necessary

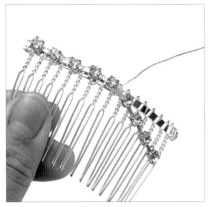

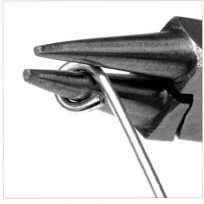

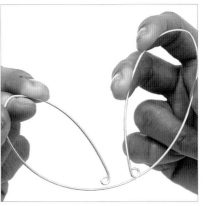

1. Take 2½ in. (6 cm) of ¼ in. (4 mm) round rhinestone chain and, with a 10 in. (25 cm) length of 24-gauge (0.5 mm) round silver-plated copper wire, wrap and secure the piece to the top section of the hair comb. Only wrap once between each rhinestone to retain sufficient space for future wire wrapping.

2. Cut a 15 in. (38 cm) length of 16-gauge (1.2 mm) round silver-colored copper wire straight from a coil, maintaining the curve of the wire. Use round-nose pliers to create a loop of about ¼ in. (5 mm) outer diameter. Bend the loop end with your fingers, following the original curve. Bring the loop backward toward the center of the wire, roughly 8 in. (20 cm) from the end.

3. Use round-nose pliers to loop the other end of the wire; make the loop smaller than the opposite end, with an outer diameter of approximately ⅛ in. (4 mm). Using your fingers, again shape this other looped wire end in toward the center so two leaflike shapes are created.

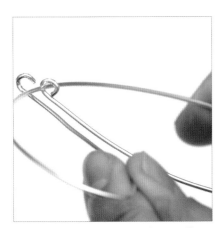

4. Use flat-, chain-, or curved-nose pliers to open both loops before inserting the center of the wire to connect the parts together, then close the loops to secure. The openings of both loops should be facing the back of the piece, with the larger "leaf" shape on the right-hand side.

5. Wind 10 in. (25 cm) of 24-gauge (0.5 mm) round silver-coated wire in between the spaces of the rhinestone chain to bind the wire shape to the top of the hair comb. Once the wire is fixed around the final rhinestone, secure the wire in place by winding it around a few times. Cut away any excess and squeeze with pliers.

Tip: As the area of the frame is quite substantial to cover with wire, in order to keep lengths of 24-gauge (0.5 mm) winding wire from becoming knotted or kinked, use two lengths of approximately 18 in. (45 cm). Any longer and it will become cumbersome to wrap around the frame.

Continues on next page

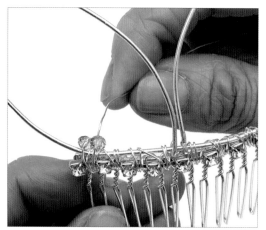

6. Starting at the left, wrap 4 mm round faceted natural-colored beads along the top of the comb where the wire shape is joined, using 10 in. (25 cm) of 24-gauge (0.5 mm) round wire. When the last bead has been secured, wind the wire around the frame a few more times before cutting away the excess wire. Squeeze the wire end with pliers to secure.

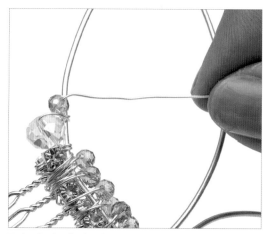

7. Again, beginning from the left-hand side, cover the leaf-shaped frame by wire-wrapping (see page 62) a mix of 4 mm natural-colored and 8 mm clear faceted beads along the wire using 24-gauge (0.5 mm) round wire. During the wrapping of the beads, make sure a slight gap is left at the top, right-hand corner of the left-hand leaf shape.

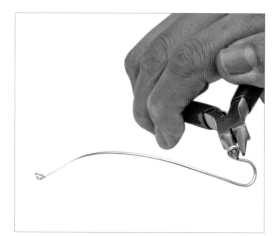

8. At the end of the remaining 16-gauge (1.2 mm) round silver-coated copper wire, create a loop that has an outer diameter of about ⅛ in. (4 mm). Shape the wire with your fingers into a curve that is approximately 1¼ in. (3 cm) high at the tallest part, in the center. Curve the end around the jaws of the round-nose pliers before making a loop at the end.

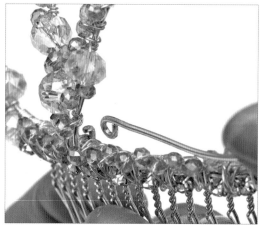

9. Connect the loop of this curved wire piece to the larger first loop of the "leaf" frame, positioning it at the back of the comb by carefully opening the large loop at the back. Join the two loops before closing the loop of the frame to connect them securely. Bind and secure with approximately 8 in. (20 cm) of 24-gauge (0.5 mm) round wire around both loops for added security of the two parts.

10. After connecting the leaf frame to the comb, reshape it with your fingers and pliers if the piece has become slightly distorted. Position the other end of the curved wire piece at the slight gap on the top corner of the right-hand leaf wire shape. Secure it in place by binding it with 8 in. (20 cm) of 24-gauge (0.5 mm) round wire.

11. Cover the curved wire by securing a 4 in. (10 cm) length of ⅛ in. (3.5 mm) round rhinestone chain. Do so with a 10 in. (25 cm) length of 24-gauge (0.5 mm) round wire, winding it around the rhinestone chain and along the length of the wire to secure the two together.

12. Create four small drop charms with chain, head pins, and jump rings, and 4 mm and 8 mm faceted beads. The chain drop is created with one head pin, one 5 mm jump ring, ¾ in. (2 cm) of ⅛ in. (2.5 mm) chain, and one 4 mm and one 8 mm faceted bead. The remaining drops are created by threading beads through a head pin and creating a looped end, before winding the end to close.

13. Open the loop at the front of the curved piece with flat-nose pliers and connect the four crystal bead drops. Close the loop with pliers to secure the four drops in place.

Brooch

Brooches are often forgotten about when it comes to thinking of desirable jewelry pieces to design and make. However, they can be fun, contemporary, and worn on everyday outfits or to adorn a special outfit, scarf, or even a hat.

The basis of making a brooch was illustrated earlier in the book (see pages 44–45). It must have a sharp pin that can pierce material or clothing, and the pin requires a spring-type mechanism. With both of these features in place, any design and wire form can be applied to the front of the pin—although you must think about the weight and weight distribution of the piece to allow it to balance and sit evenly on the wearer.

During the design process, always consider the position of the pin in conjunction with the main feature of the brooch—where it will be located, how it will sit against the clothing, and whether it will hang naturally. Finally, remember that when the brooch is worn the pin should thread away from the wearer to avoid injury.

Claw settings are commonly associated with fine jewelry to hold and secure a stone or bead. The addition of threaded wire through the center of a bead offers additional security; as illustrated in this project, this method, combined with the shaped claw setting, provides a durable way of securing the main bead.

You will need:

» 27½ in. (70 cm) of 18-gauge (1 mm) round, gold-colored copper wire
» Approximately 63 in. (160 cm) of 24-gauge (0.5 mm) round, gold-colored copper wire
» 1 large faceted bead with central vertically drilled 2.5 mm hole, approximately 1½ × 1 in. (40 x 25 mm)
» 10 teardrop beads with horizontally drilled holes, ½ × ¼ in. (12 × 6 mm)
» Ruler or tape measure
» Wire cutters
» Ring clamp or masking tape
» Nylon-coated flat-nose pliers
» Chain-nose pliers
» Ring-nose pliers
» Fine-jaw pliers
» Planishing hammer
» Flat metal stake
» Jewelry file
» Emery stick and paper

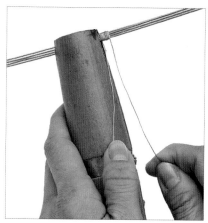

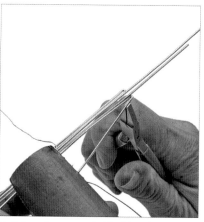

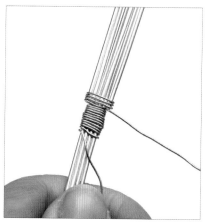

1. Cut three 6¼ in. (16 cm) lengths and one 8¾ in. (22 cm) length of 18-gauge (1 mm) tempered wire, and gather so they are parallel. Secure together, with the long piece in the second position, into a ring clamp or with masking tape. Wind an 18 in. (45 cm) length of 24-gauge (0.5 mm) round gold-colored copper wire to secure the wires at the center point. Wind a ¼ in. (6 mm) width.

2. If the wires were held with a ring clamp, remove and reposition the bound ¼ in. (6 mm) section so the end sits flush with the end of the clamp. Measure one of the outer four wires 1¼ in. (3.5 cm) along from the edge of the clamp. Using flat-nose pliers, make a bend to the side at this position. Bend the wire back around itself. Repeat the process with the opposite wire.

3. Place the piece back into the ring clamp, with the double-bend wire section inserted and held in place. Allow part of it to protrude, and then, taking the winding 24-gauge (0.5 mm) wire, continue to bind, encasing and wrapping the two ends. Cover a length of approximately ¼ in. (8 mm) so the double wires are secured in place.

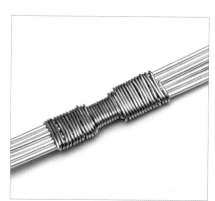

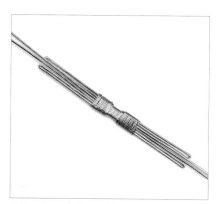

4. Remove the piece from the ring clamp and repeat steps 2 and 3 with the two outer wires on the opposite side. Again, wrap another length of approximately ¼ in. (8 mm) so that the double wires are secured. (All four double wires are now secured in place.) Cut and remove any excess 24-gauge (0.5 mm) wrapping wire.

5. The bound piece will now look like this, with four double wire sections, one 6¼ in. (16 cm), and one 8¾ in. (22 cm) wire, all of which are secured together with the central 24-gauge (0.5 mm) coiled-wire section.

6. With the wound ends facing inward, thread a large, faceted, opaque stone onto the 8¾ in. (22 cm) length of wire until approximately ⅜ in. (1 cm) from the edge of the bound wire section. Pull the bead forward, bringing the stone and wire forward as well. Continue to pull the stone forward until it sits flat against the wound wires.

Continues on next page

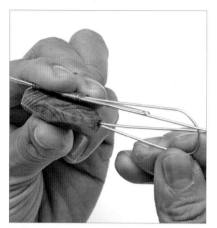

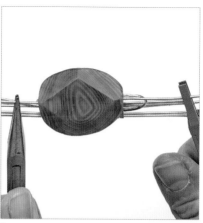

7. Curve the opposite end of the wire under the bead with your fingers and pliers before guiding the wire upward into the base entrance of the bead hole. Insert and push the wire from the base until it appears at the top hole. Gently pull upward.

8. Pull on the top and bottom wires as tightly as possible with two pairs of pliers. Continue to tug until both wire ends are tight in order to secure the bead in place.

9. Use flat-nose pliers to move the four double wires until they are slightly pulled apart and angled. With your fingers, guide each piece over the top of the bead. Gently push it forward and move each to the front of the bead with your fingers and fine-jaw pliers.

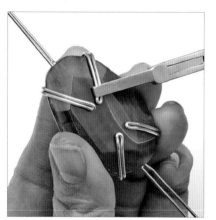

10. Continue to use fine flat-nose pliers to pull the wire ends downward, closer to the surface of the bead. Use your fingers to manipulate until the wire ends are as close to the front of the bead as possible.

11. Take the wire from the top of the bead and pull it backward so it meets the last remaining 6¼ in. (16 cm) length of wire. Wrap the wire around this remaining length of wire, cut away any excess, and secure by pressing tightly with flat-nose pliers.

12. At the front of the piece, take the bottom wire protruding from the bead hole and create an irregularly sided triangle shape with flat-nose pliers. Wind the wire end of the shape around the top of the triangle at the base of the bead to secure in place. Cut away and remove any excess wire.

13. Bend the top of the remaining length of wire at the back so it sits perpendicular to the bead. Then use round-nose pliers to create a double-coil spring mechanism, as illustrated on pages 44–45.

14. Take the remaining opposite wire end and, using flat-nose pliers, also bend this so it sits perpendicular to the stone. Both wire ends will protrude upward from the base of the bead.

15. Use the flat-nose pliers to form a rectangular-shaped hook before cutting away any excess wire with the wire cutters. Cut the wire end so there is an opening in the hook, leaving sufficient space to insert the pin of the brooch.

16. The pin of the brooch can be connected and secured in place by the rectangular-shaped hook clasp. The pin can be hammered, tapered, and filed to a point, as shown on page 44, with the use of a planishing hammer, files, and emery stick and paper.

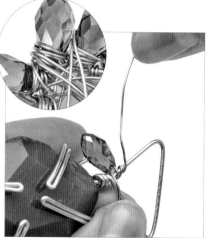

17. At the front, wind and secure the drop beads with 20 in. (50 cm) of 24-gauge (0.5 mm) round wire. Thread the wire through the hole of the drop bead and then wrap it around the wire frame of the triangle shape. Once all the drop beads have been secured, use a 20 in. (50 cm) length of 24-gauge (0.5 mm) wire to wrap around the base of each bead to secure them.

18. Wrap a second 20 in. (50 cm) length of 24-gauge (0.5 mm) round wire, crisscrossing around the triangle shape. This will offer security, and will give a more three-dimensional frame. Cut away excess wire, but leave a 1/8–3/8 in. (5–10 mm) end, which can be threaded into the main body of the wire frame at the back and tucked away discreetly.

French-knit bangle

French-knit pieces can have a rather traditional, crafted quality; however, simple changes such as the color of the wire and using unfussy embellishments and findings can transform the look to give a sharper, more stylish finish. The main body of the bangle is a simple length of French-knit wire; the square-profile wire cage creates clean lines and edges, adding to the aesthetic appeal.

To give the bangle a modern aesthetic, a white-colored coated wire has been selected—and by coupling this with a matching simple wire cage, a contemporary style is achieved.

During the design process, the findings of a piece should be considered—too often, these are neglected. The clasp fitting of this bangle replicates the square shape of the central wire cube, and the angular look has been preserved. The addition of the machine-made caps and beads masks any unsightly wire ends here, giving a professional finish. Do not be concerned about using store-bought findings; a unique handmade piece does not have to be produced entirely from handcrafted components.

Finally, by creating the piece in two parts the wearer is able to detach and wear the pieces separately—the square frame can be suspended from a chain on the neck, while the French-knit bangle can be worn on its own or threaded with other components.

You will need:

- » 79 in. (200 cm) of 24-gauge (0.5 mm) round, white-coated copper wire
- » 10 in. (25 cm) of 16-gauge (1.2 mm) round, silver-coated copper wire for the clasp and end
- » 14 in. (35 cm) of 19-gauge (0.9 mm) square-profile, silver-coated copper wire
- » 2 silver-plated end caps, ⅜ × ⅜ in. (10 × 10 mm)
- » 4 × 5 mm round, hollow, silver-plated beads
- » French-knitting tool
- » Crochet hook
- » Wire cutters
- » Tape measure or ruler
- » Flat nylon-coated pliers
- » Fine flat-nose pliers
- » Chain-nose pliers
- » Round-nose pliers
- » Curved-nose pliers

CREATE THE BANGLE

Tip: The amount of wire given to create the French-knit bangle is approximate, and is based on an average-sized person. To work out the approximate length of wire you require, know that 2 in. (5 cm) of wire makes approximately ⅜ in. (1 cm) of the knit—however, this will vary depending on the tools you use and how tightly you knit.

1. Create a 6½ in. (17 cm) length of French knit (see pages 84–85), using an estimated 55 in. (140 cm) of 24-gauge (0.5 mm) round, white-coated copper wire. Leave roughly 8 in. (20 cm) of wire free at each end. Cut two 5 in. (12.5 cm) lengths of 16-gauge (1.2 mm) round wire, and make a small loop on the end of each. Make the loops as small and as neat as possible. Insert the wire from the non-looped end into the knit and up, ¼ in. (5 mm) from one end.

2. Using the 8 in. (20 cm) white wire end, secure the looped wire piece to the French-knit length by threading it through the loop and winding to secure it in place. Continue to thread and wind to "sew" the two parts together, until there are no gaps in the loop.

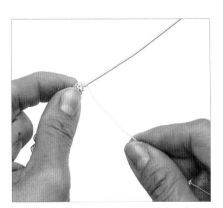

3. Once the two parts are secured, bring the wire to the top and wind it around the central wire three or four times. Cut excess wire with wire cutters and secure by squeezing the end with pliers.

4. Thread through one end cap and allow it to drop over the top of the French-knit length, covering the looped and bound parts. Continue by threading two hollow beads, and leave a small gap of approximately ⅛ in. (3 mm) before using flat-nose pliers to make a right-angle bend on the central wire.

5. Using flat-nose pliers, create a ½ in. (12 mm) square above the two hollow beads, then wrap wire around below the square to secure it in place. Cut away any excess wire and secure further by squeezing the end with pliers.

Continues on next page

CREATE THE CUBE FRAME

6. Repeat steps 2, 3, and 4 on the opposite side of the French knit before making a matching ½ in. (12 mm) square frame, but instead of wrapping the wire end around the base, guide it into the frame and create two more bends. Cut away any excess wire if necessary.

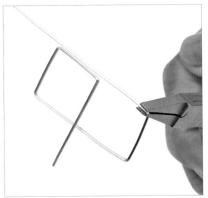

1. Straighten and temper a length of 19-gauge (0.9 mm) square-profile wire with flat nylon-coated pliers before cutting a 6¾ in. (17 cm) length. Leave 1½ in. (4 cm) from the wire end before using fine, sharp, flat-nose pliers to make a double square-shaped frame. Each square should measure approximately ¾ × ¾ in. (20 × 20 mm) and they should sit side by side. Approximately 1½ in. (4 cm) of wire will extend from the end.

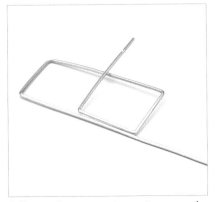

2. Repeat the process to create a second double square shape, taking care to measure and match it with the first shaped frame.

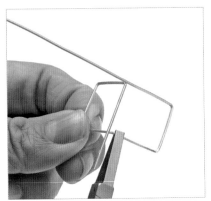

3. Place the flat-nose pliers at the center point of the frame, with the shorter extended wire end sitting to the left of the jaws. Using your fingers, bend the left-hand square frame downward. Continue to gently tease the frame backward until the right-hand side reaches a right angle and the piece becomes a two-sided frame.

4. Repeat step 3 with the second piece until both are matching. Make sure the sides are at right angles and are square. If any of the lines are misshapen or off, use your fingers and flat-nose pliers to straighten them.

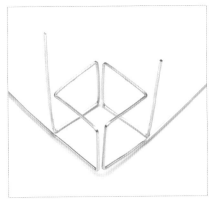

5. Position the two pieces so they sit together neatly and close together to form an open square frame. Adjust with your fingers and pliers if necessary to fit the two parts together as neatly as possible. Take time to adjust at this stage before the two parts are connected together, as once they are joined it will be difficult to reshape them.

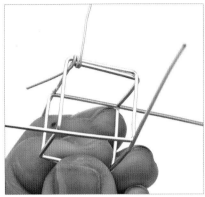

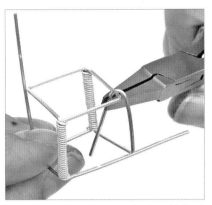

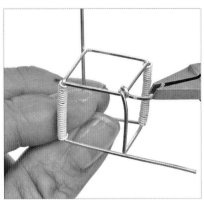

6. Cut a 20 in. (50 cm) length of 24-gauge (0.5 mm) round wire and, while holding the two frames together, wrap around the two edges that meet between the half-squares. Bind from one side to the other along the length of the two wire edges. Repeat on the opposite wire edges to join the two parts together with another 20 in. (50 cm) length of 24-gauge (0.5 mm) wire.

7. Once the two parts are wired and joined together, a square frame is created. Reshape with your fingers and pliers if necessary to ensure straight edges and right angles. Remove excess wire on all four protruding wire pieces if necessary, so the wire ends are approximately ¾ in. (2 cm) long. Using curved-nose or fine flat-nose pliers, take hold of one of the loose wires at the edge and bend it inward, into the cube.

8. Hold and wrap the wire around the square frame, securing it in place. With wire cutters, remove any excess wire before squeezing the end. Repeat this for two other wire ends, leaving one. Take care when doing this wrap around that the edges of the cube remain straight and are not angled or pulled downward. Also, do not pull too tightly, as you want to avoid crushing the frame.

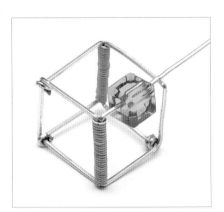

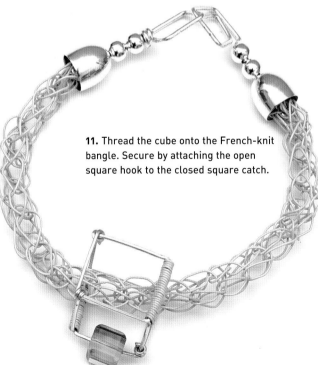

9. Once three of the wires are wrapped and secured, there will be one wire end remaining. Thread one square bead onto the last wire piece before wrapping and securing the wire end in place as shown in steps 7 and 8. Cut away any excess wire with wire cutters and squeeze the end with chain-nose pliers.

10. The finished cage piece is strong and secure. It can be threaded onto any piece at various angles and positions through the framework.

11. Thread the cube onto the French-knit bangle. Secure by attaching the open square hook to the closed square catch.

Bird's nest necklace

This charming necklace is simple and quick to produce. Composed of five individual "bird's nest" components, the striking central feature makes for a strong but lightweight and comfortable jewelry piece.

The wire nest device frames the beads perfectly, and by finishing the piece with matching pearls and ribbon you can add a contemporary touch. Each individual "bird's nest" component is unique, and you can create variations by using different sizes and types of beads or wire. For example, using gold-colored wire and adding richer tones of beads—such as ruby red—will create a really opulent piece.

This is an attractive project with a technique that requires few tools. No jigs are necessary, and the wire is shaped and manipulated by hand. The ease of production makes this design ideal for the creation of matching jewelry sets of earrings, bracelets, and rings; the design possibilities are endless.

The individual nests do not require accurate measurements. As each nest component follows an organic aesthetic, a slight change in the length of wire used or the coiling of the wire around the beads will not have an adverse effect; quite the opposite, in fact.

You will need:
- » 126 in. (320 cm) of 20-gauge (0.8 mm) round, silver-plated copper wire
- » 7 × 6 mm pearls
- » 9 × 5 mm faceted crystal beads
- » 4 × 8 mm pearls
- » 12 in. (30 cm) of 0.45 mm tiger tail wire
- » 4 × 4 mm silver-plated wire guards
- » 2 × 2 mm crimps
- » 60 × 5 mm pearls
- » 2 × 4 mm silver-plated crimp covers
- » 19 in. (48 cm) of ⅛ in. (4 mm) ribbon
- » 2 × 4 mm ribbon caps
- » 2 × 5 mm silver-plated split rings
- » Tape measure or ruler
- » Wire cutters
- » Round-nose pliers
- » Flat- or tapered-nose pliers
- » Curved-nose pliers

1. Measure and cut 20 in. (50 cm) of 20-gauge (0.8 mm) round wire and create a small loop at the end with round-nose pliers. Make the loop as small and as discreet as possible by using the tip of the pliers' jaws.

2. Thread one small pearl and two of the faceted beads along to the loop. Holding the piece with your forefinger and thumb, rotate in a clockwise direction and start to wind the beads so the wire begins to curve around.

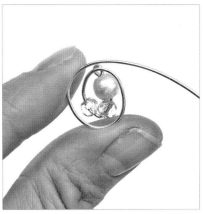

3. Continue to wind and rotate the piece with one hand while holding the wire end with the other. While rotating the piece, feed the wire around so the piece starts to form and become larger and more "nestlike."

4. When approximately 5–6 in. (12–15 cm) of wire is remaining, take flat- or tapered-nose pliers and make a right angle close to the wire nest piece. The wire will now sit perpendicular to the wire nest frame.

5. Grip the wire end with your fingers and guide it forward over the front of the nest frame, before threading it through the piece and the original loop. Pull the wire through to the back and wrap it around the frame twice, then bring the wire up to the top of the nest shape.

6. With round-nose pliers, hold the wire just above the top of the nest frame, then wrap it around twice to create a double loop. Close and secure the double loop by wrapping the wire end around twice below. Cut off any excess wire with wire cutters and secure by squeezing with pliers.

Continues on next page

7. Repeat steps 1 to 6, using a single large pearl to complete a second loop-ended bird's nest frame component.

8. Make three more bird's nest frames by following steps 1 to 3, using 16 in. (40 cm) of 20-gauge (0.8 mm) round wire; however at the end, instead of creating a double loop, use round-nose pliers to make a matching small loop. Open the end loop with curved-nose pliers and connect with the first loop. Use pliers to close loops securely before manipulating the two to ensure they are neat and as hidden behind the wire "nest" frame as possible.

9. Upon completion of all five bird's nest frames, set each piece in the desired configuration—remember, the two looped components must sit at either end to allow for further connection.

10. Once you have decided on an arrangement, take the first bird's nest frame from the left-hand side and, with an 8 in. (20 cm) length of 20-gauge (0.8 mm) round wire, leave ⅜ in. (1 cm) before securing and wrapping at the join location with the next bird's nest frame. Wrap the wire around the frame twice to secure it.

11. Hold the second bird's nest frame next to the first before guiding the wire below the piece. Bring the wire upward and around the frame, and again wrap it around twice. Repeat the wrapping process back around the first frame again, and complete by wrapping the second bird's nest twice.

12. Bring both wire ends to the back, and wrap the long piece around the shorter piece twice, then cut away any excess wire. Cut the remaining wire so it is ⅜ in. (1 cm) long prior to making the smallest loop. Squeeze and manipulate the two parts with fine round-nose pliers so they are discreetly hidden at the back.

13. Repeat the wrapping process until all five bird's nests have been secured together, with the looped versions on either end. The piece should be sitting in a slight curve to follow the natural curve of the neck.

14. Using the technique shown on page 99, take a length of tiger tail, thread it through a wire guard and a crimp, and connect it to the right-hand looped nest frame. Crimp and secure it in place before threading on 30 pearls. Thread on a wire guard and crimp at the end of the length of the beads, then crimp to secure.

15. Cover all four crimps with crimp covers. Repeat step 14 on the opposite side of the piece, and again cover all four crimps with crimp covers. Once the length of pearls has been secured and completed, connect 11 in. (28 cm) of ribbon with ribbon end caps, as shown on page 102. Complete the piece by threading one large bead onto both ribbon ends and secure in place by tying a knot below and above the pearls.

16. The completed neckpiece can be worn by tying the ribbon securely around the neck to achieve the desired length.

Chapter Four:

Pattern Directory

The following directory comprises wire shapes and patterns, which are achieved using a wire jig or created freehand with the assistance of pliers. To replicate each, start at arrow 1 and trace the wire over the actual-size diagram, following each arrow in the order and direction indicated.

The chapter is broken into two parts, with the jig-formed pieces illustrated at the beginning, followed by the freehand patterns. Approximately 8–12 in. (200–300 mm) of 20-gauge (0.80 mm) copper wire has been used to create each design, but the size of the finished pieces and the size and type of wire can be easily altered to personal choice. Remember to add a bit of excess wire to allow the part to be held during the shaping process, and practice to work out the amount of wire required before creating your final piece.

JIG PATTERNS

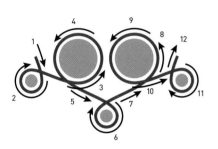

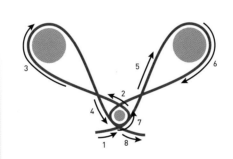

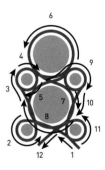

Multi-loop
Follow the jig pattern. This can form the centerpiece of a necklace or links in a handmade chain. Parts can be attached to and suspended from the three smaller loops.

Sycamore
Follow the jig pattern. Once shaped, wrap one wire end around the other to secure the central loop. Thread a bead onto the remaining wire end and use round-nose pliers to make a closed loop.

Turtle
Follow the jig pattern. To complete, shape one wire end into a round loop and secure by winding the other wire around the loop base. This shape works well for a clasp end.

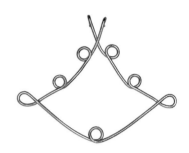

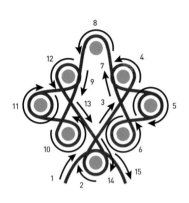

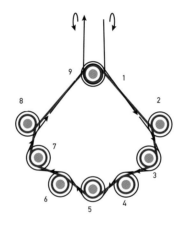

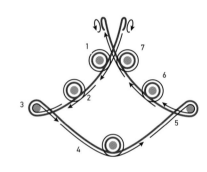

Nouveau
Follow the jig pattern. Connect beads, chain, and additional wire parts to the multiple loops of this piece.

Bellflower
Follow the jig pattern. Once shaped, use round-nose pliers to loop the two wire ends. This is a great component for a necklace or drop earrings.

Pearl
Follow the jig pattern. Use round-nose pliers to loop each wire end. These loops allow the piece to connect to other parts and provide a point for suspension.

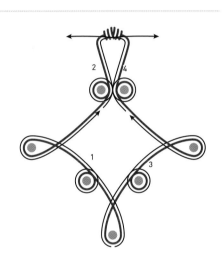

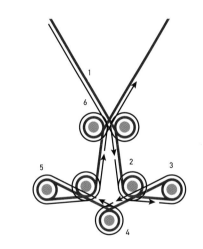

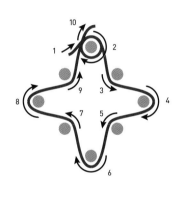

Celtic Twist
Follow the jig pattern. Secure the wire ends by wrapping them around each other. Add beads to the loops of the "V"–shaped base to create a pendant. Chain can be connected to the top by adding a jump or split ring.

Swallow
Follow the jig pattern. Finish by looping the wire ends with round-nose pliers. This design can be created in various sizes and linked to produce an interesting pendant feature.

North Star
Follow the jig pattern. To finish, use round-nose pliers to make a loop from one wire end and secure by wrapping the remaining wire end around the loop base. Create and connect smaller and larger versions of this piece to make an interesting pendant.

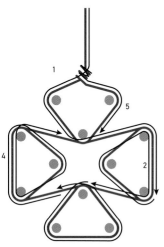

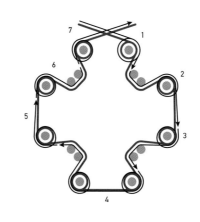

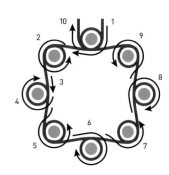

Four-Leaf Clover
Follow the jig pattern. To complete, wrap one wire end around the other. Connect several of these components together to create a suspended pendant.

Open Cross
Follow the jig pattern. Secure the wire ends by wrapping them around each other. This piece can be easily attached to a necklace or charm bracelet.

Square Frame
Follow the jig pattern. The four internal loops strengthen this square frame, while the four external loops provide connection points. To finish, wrap the two wire ends around each other or cut away the excess wire.

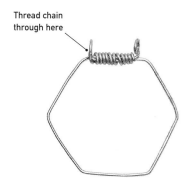

Thread chain through here

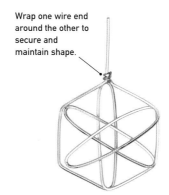

Wrap one wire end around the other to secure and maintain shape.

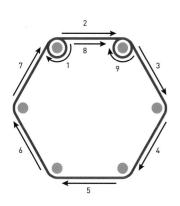

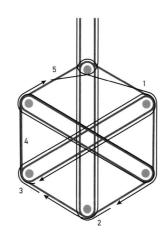

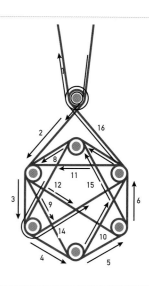

Hexagon
Follow the jig pattern. Once shaped, use pliers to manipulate the two internal loops so both sit above the piece facing each other. Secure in place by wrapping the two wire ends around the top of the pentagon.

Ellipses
Follow the jig pattern. Once shaped, wrap one wire end around the other. Suspend beads from the base of this piece to create a pendant.

Cradle
Follow the jig pattern. Secure the wire ends by wrapping one around the other. Use round-nose pliers to make a closed loop end.

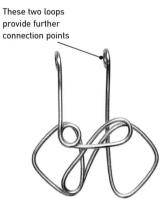

These two loops provide further connection points

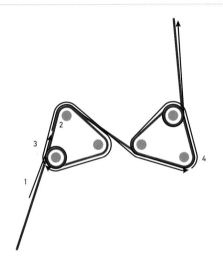

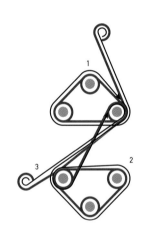

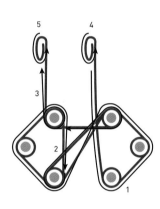

Hourglass
Follow the jig pattern. To complete, loop the two wire ends with round-nose pliers. Link a number of these identical shapes to create a handcrafted chain.

Abstract I
Follow the jig pattern. Use round-nose pliers to loop the wire ends. Cut away any excess wire. This versatile piece can be used in earrings, necklaces, and bracelets.

Abstract II
Follow the jig pattern. This wire shape can be utilized for many jewelry items. Individual parts can be used for earrings or multiple loops may be connected to form a bracelet or necklace chain.

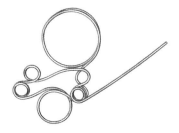

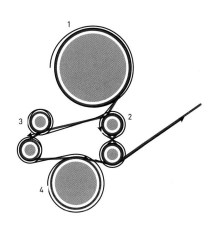

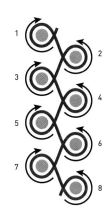

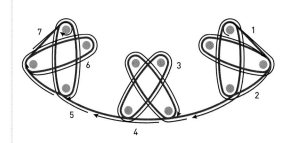

Ribbon
Follow the jig pattern. Use round-nose pliers to shape a hook or a closed loop in the wire end. Cut away any excess wire to finish.

Scroll
Follow the jig pattern. This is an ideal piece for connecting and suspending beads, chain, and other wire components. The open-ended loops at either end of the piece provide intial connection points.

Orion
Follow the jig pattern. Once shaped, cut away any excess wire. Connect chain to the small loops at each end to make a necklace, or link three identical pieces to produce a detailed collar effect.

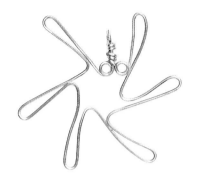

FREEHAND PATTERNS

Use round-nose pliers to curve the hands and feet forward

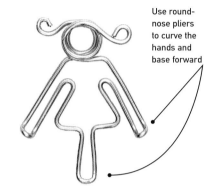

Use round-nose pliers to curve the hands and base forward

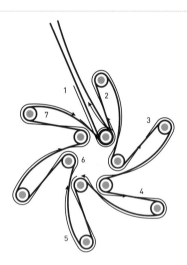

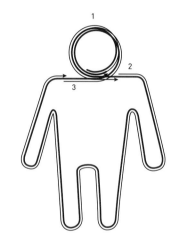

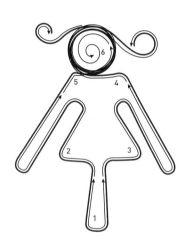

Catherine Wheel

Follow the jig pattern. Wrap the wire ends around each other to secure in place. This shape is ideal for use as a pendant or brooch piece.

Man

Using round-nose pliers, wrap the wire around the largest part of the jaws of the pliers once to create the head. Once the head shape is achieved, guide the wire to the right, following the curve of the shoulder before continuing to shape the body. Bring the wire around the original head shape to complete.

Woman

Shape this figure with round-nose pliers. Create a three-dimensional effect by gripping and rotating the hands and base forward with round-nose pliers.

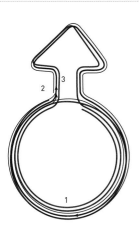

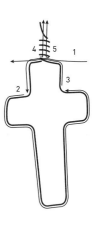

Mars

Wind a long length of wire around a ring mandrel to create a large loop. Use flat-nose pliers to create the arrowhead. The finished piece can be thread through a chain to create a pendant, or made from heavier gauge wire to create finger rings.

Venus

Wind a long length of wire around a ring mandrel to create a large loop. Use flat-nose pliers to create the right-angle bends of the cross feature. Use round-nose pliers to add decorative loops to the top of the cross feature. The finished piece can be thread through a chain to create a pendant, or made from heavier gauge wire to create finger rings.

Cross

Use flat-nose pliers to create the square corners of this cross. Once shaped, bend both wire ends upward and wrap one end around the other. Create a closed loop end with round-nose pliers and secure in place. The finished piece can be applied as a charm to a necklace or bracelet (see pages 116–119).

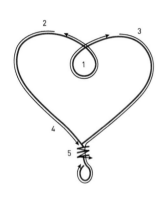

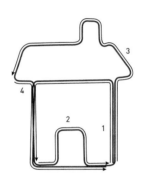

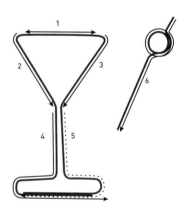

Heart

Form the first central loop with round-nose pliers and use half-round pliers, flat-nose pliers, and your fingers to shape the rest of the heart. Wrap one wire end around the other and cut away the excess wire. Create a loop with the remaining wire end and wrap the end around twice to secure in place. See pages 116–119 for instructions on using this motif as part of a charm bracelet.

House

Make this house shape with very fine-tipped flat-nose pliers. A chain, jump ring, or split ring can be connected through the top of the "house" shape.

Cocktail Glass and Stick

Form the sharp corners of this glass with chain- or flat-nose pliers. Use round-nose pliers to shape the base of the glass and the cocktail stick. Link the two parts together with a chain or jump ring.

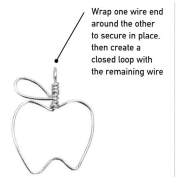

Wrap one wire end around the other to secure in place, then create a closed loop with the remaining wire

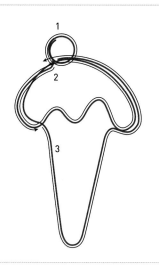

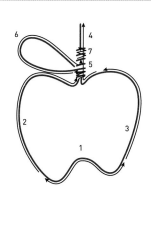

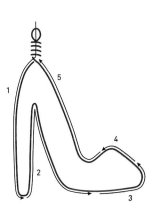

Ice Cream Cone

Starting with a double loop, use round-nose pliers to create the shape of this ice cream cone. The finished piece can be applied as a charm to a necklace or bracelet.

Apple

Shape the body of this apple charm with half-round- or flat-nose pliers. Use round-nose pliers to create a leaf shape in one wire end and wrap this around the other wire end to create a stalk. Use round-nose pliers to make a closed loop-end connection point.

Shoe

Create the tight bends of this shoe heel with chain-nose pliers and use half-round- or flat-nose pliers to make the softer curve of the outsole. Form the remaining toe bends with round-nose pilers. Make a closed loop end with round-nose pliers to complete the piece.

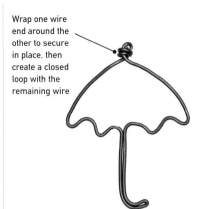

Wrap one wire end around the other to secure in place, then create a closed loop with the remaining wire

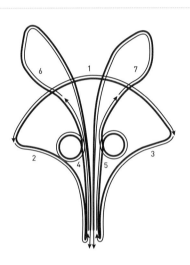

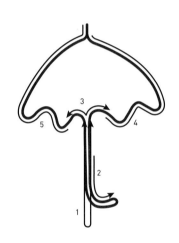

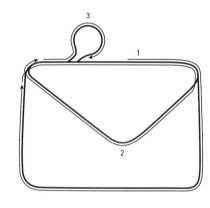

Fox
Use round- and half-round-nose pliers to create this fox shape. To finish, loop the two wire ends with round-nose pliers. Thread and suspend the complete shape from a chain or attach jump or split rings to link it to another wire part.

Umbrella
Using round-nose pliers, bend the length of wire so that the two ends run parallel to each other. Use round-nose pliers to shape the handle. Shape the umbrella canopy and wrap one wire end around the other to secure in place. Create a closed loop with the remaining wire end. The finished piece is an ideal necklace or bracelet charm and can be connected by the closed loop.

Envelope
Create this envelope with flat-nose pliers. Use round-nose pliers to form the connection loop.

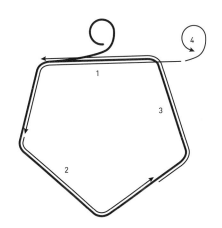

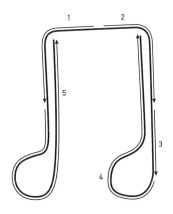

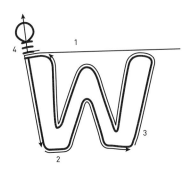

Pentagon

Create the angles of this pentagon with chain- and flat-nose pliers. Use round-nose pliers to form the final loop. Link this individual shape by the loop, connect several together to create a chain, or make a necklace feature by combining different sizes.

Music Note

Start from the center of the wire and use flat-nose pliers to shape the corners of the top bar. Create the remaining bends with round-nose pliers. Thread a jump or split ring through the top bar to provide a connection point.

Letter

Create a useful guide by sketching your letter shape on paper. Form the letter and join the two wire ends by wrapping one around the other. Complete by making a closed loop end. See pages 116–119 for further instructions on creating this charm.

Index

Credits

Quarto would like to thank the following for kindly supplying images for inclusion in this book:

Entwistle, Rachel, **www.rachelentwistle.co.uk**, p.11br
Meyer, Gosia, **www.gosiameyerjewelry.com**, p.13t
Poupazis, Chris & Joy, **www.cjpoupazis.com**, p.11bc
Scantlebury, Simon, **www.simonscantlebury.com**, p.11bl
West, Terry, **www.oceansdreamingdesigns.com**, p.11tr

All step-by-step and other images are the copyright of Quarto Publishing plc. While every effort has been made to credit contributors, Quarto would like to apologize should there have been any omissions or errors—and would be pleased to make the appropriate correction for future editions of the book.

Thanks to Cookson Precious Metals Ltd
for providing images of tools and materials.

Cookson Precious Metals Ltd
59-83 Vittoria Street
Birmingham B1 3NZ
United Kingdom
0121 200 2120
www.cooksongold.com

Author Acknowledgments
A special thanks to Jason, Dylan, and Rhys.

Further Information
The information supplied in this book is accurate and true to the best of my knowledge. All safety procedures have been considered, but we cannot guarantee avoidance of any injuries that may occur while using the techniques in this book. Jewelry making poses some dangers. It is at the reader's own risk to follow and apply the techniques demonstrated.

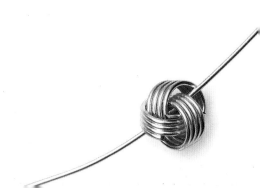